This
I Believe

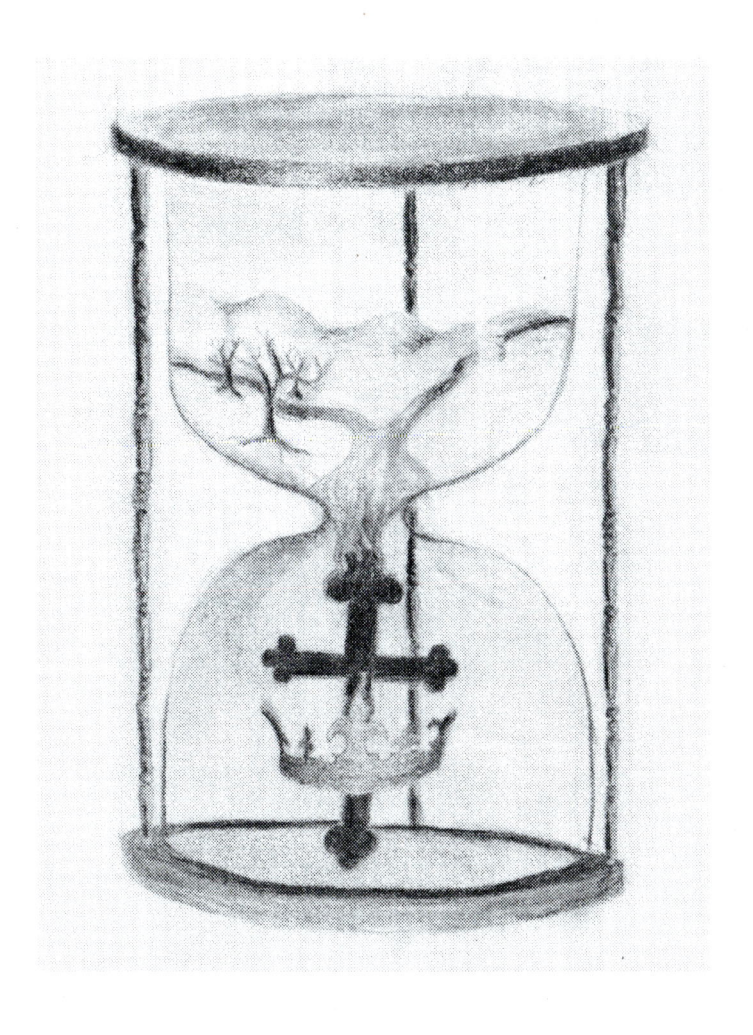

H. Burnham Kirkland

This I Believe

Copyright @ 1998
H. Burnham Kirkland

All rights reserved.
No part of this book may be
reproduced in any form, except for
the inclusion of brief quotations in a review
or article, without permission in writing
from the author or publisher.

ISBN 0-7392-0031-3

Library of Congress Catalog Card
Number 98-094133

Quotations from the Bible,
unless otherwise indicated, are from the
Revised Standard Version of The Holy Bible
Copyright 1946, 1952
by the Division of Christian Education of the
National Council of Churches of Christ in the U.S.A.

Additional copies are available.
For your convenience an order form may
be found at the back of this book.

Published by
Kirkland Books
2425 Harden Blvd, #265
Lakeland, Fl. 33803-5956

Printed in the USA by

MP
MORRIS PUBLISHING

3212 East Highway 30 • Kearney, NE 68847 • 1-800-650-7888

This volume is dedicated
with love to my grandchildren,
Christofer Dennis Rasmussen
and Jessica Elizabeth Rasmussen.

Fellow Searchers for the Truth that sets us free.
(John 8:32)

Cover Drawing is by Jessica Elizabeth Rasmussen age eighteen, granddaughter of the author. Here is her interpretation of her work entitled, "Time and Eternity."

"The hour glass represents time. The upper chamber contains the sands of time, two converging paths, and leafless trees. The leafless trees represent the end of a cycle of life. The two converging paths stand for individual spirituality. We each take our own path in finding our spirituality, but in the end we all wind up in the same place. This realization is shown in the drawing by the sands of time falling and the two paths converging. The sand then enters the lower chamber containing a symbol of God and becomes a part of the symbol much the same way we are all part of the Higher Power."

J.E.R.

Table of Contents

Do Our Beliefs Matter? 1
Christianity 9
How To Find God 19
The Uniqueness of Jesus 33
The Power Of The Holy Spirit 51
What Do We Believe About The Trinity? 61
What Is A Sacrament? 71
The Bible—The Word Of God 79
Prayer In The Christian Life 89
The Church—Who Needs It? 101
The Importance of Sunday School 111
Spiritual Healing 119
The Kingdom Of God 129
You Must Forgive To Be Forgiven 137
What About Judgement? 149
Dealing With The Devil 157
Life After Death 165
I Thought You'd Never Ask 173
He Is Risen 183
Uncertainty In Religion 191

Chapter 1

Do Our Beliefs Matter?

The opening words of the average person's creed would probably read something like this: "It doesn't really matter what a person believes. It's the life he or she lives that really counts." If one participates in many discussions about religious topics, one constantly hears the recurring theme: "Beliefs really make no practical difference in everyday life."

A surprising amount of evidence can be marshaled to support the contention that beliefs are of no practical importance. Frederick the Great once said: "I hope that posterity will distinguish the philosopher from the monarch in me." He wanted to be judged on the basis of his lofty ideas rather than the grimy decisions he made in the political arena. Frederick the Great was operating on the assumption that beliefs make no real difference in life.

Various opinion polls and sociological studies seem to indicate that, for the majority of people in our own time, beliefs have little, if any, influence on daily life. Several years ago, a nationwide poll was taken in the United States on religious questions. When asked whether they believed in God, ninety-five percent of those polled answered "yes." When asked whether religion in any way affected their politics and their business, fifty-four percent said. "no." When asked whether they tried to lead a good life as a result of their belief in God, only twenty-five percent admitted any connection between the two! The findings seem to indicate that beliefs are really rather unimportant.

Other studies have reported similar evidence. Hollingshead, an outstanding sociologist, spent a considerable amount of time in a small Midwestern town talking with teenagers about their beliefs and their conduct. His conclu-

This I Believe

sion was that, in the town he labeled Elmstown, the religious beliefs of the young people influenced the lives of only ten percent of them. Murray Ross made a study of the structure of religious beliefs of youth based on a questionnaire sample of 1935 youth and intensive interviews with one hundred young people. He remarks that it is "quite obvious that religious belief is not always matched by religious practice." For about seventy percent of the youth studied, their religion had little operational relevance. Thompson, an Anglican churchman, surveyed the congregations of several British churches. He asked the church members whether their religious beliefs influenced their behavior? Ninety percent answered "No ."

Theologians have long been concerned with the vast abyss that separates belief and action. Soren Kierkegaard turned to this theme again and again. In one of his writings he says that philosophers build lovely castles of their ideas. These castles are beautiful to behold. But when they are through thinking their noble thoughts, these thinkers leave their gorgeous castles and live their lives in a tumbled down shack by the side of the road. We all know many people like that—people whose professed beliefs are beautiful, but whose daily lives are drab and tawdry by comparison. Indeed, if we could "see ourselves as others see us," we might notice the same condition existing in us.

In the face of all this evidence which seems to indicate that beliefs are not important, the person who maintains that beliefs are important, and that convictions do count faces an uphill battle. Nevertheless, it is just this that I Believe! In the wisdom literature of the Old Testament, the seventh verse of the twenty-third chapter of the Book of Proverbs as translated in the King James Version it says: "For as he thinketh in his heart, so is he." It does not say: "as a man thinketh in the top of his mind, so is he." Rather

Do Our Beliefs Matter?

it speaks about what we believe in the depths of our being—"in his heart."

One day I watched as a new facade was being put on a drab old building. The contractor did not improve the basic structure of the old building. He merely dressed up its appearance. The building was little different than it had been before, except that it now had a beautiful front which the passing crowds could admire. This is what most of us do with our thoughts and beliefs; we don't want people to see how unattractive our belief structure really is. Instead we hide our real beliefs behind a pretty facade of beliefs which are on public display. When people ask us questions about religion, we show them the lovely facade that we have appropriated from the Christian tradition. When we are out in the rough-and-tumble world, we operate on the creed we really believe.

The old Anglo-Saxon word, "belief," literally means "what men live by." It is "what men live by" that we are referring to when we speak of the importance of what we believe. In the studies I have mentioned, most people were not describing what they really believed, but rather the ideas to which they rather lazily gave their assent.

Leslie Wetherhead described the profound difference between assent and belief. He said there is a world of difference between the truth to which the mind says 'yes' and the truth which captivates and alters the reactions of the entire personality. It is like the difference between an army passing through a country, compared to conquering and occupying a country; when they take charge managing its economy, its banks and transportation systems.

A belief is not merely an idea the mind possesses; it is an idea that possesses the mind.

When we say beliefs are important we do not mean the ideas we display to the public, but do not act upon; we do not mean ideas that merely win our half-hearted assent.

This I Believe

Neither do we mean the opinions that we form about peripheral matters. We have all heard about the medieval philosophers who spent much of their time debating about how many angels could dance on the head of a pin. Whatever conclusion they reached could hardly be considered relevant to their daily lives. There are many opinions that people hold about peripheral matters, but these opinions do not shape our lives. They are comparatively unimportant.

Once we have made these qualifications we can readily see that the things a person believes in their heart are crucially important.

It was not a fuzzy-headed idealist, but a very influential economist, Keynes, who said:

"The ideas of economists and political philosophers, both when they are right and when they are wrong, are more powerful than is commonly understood. Indeed, the world is ruled by little else...Practical men, who believe themselves to be quite exempt from any intellectual influences, are usually the slave of some defunct economist...I am sure that the power of vested interests is vastly exaggerated compared with the gradual encroachment of ideas...(It) is ideas, not vested interests, that are dangerous for good or evil."

In the aggressive world of business and power politics beliefs are important! Picture the struggle for power in one of the underdeveloped nations of the world. Out of the chaos of conflicting personalities there emerges one leader who seems to be gaining control of the country. The man is brilliant, a tremendous administrator, untouched by corruption. He seems to have all of the qualifications necessary. Then he states his platform: "I am a Communist." It's only a belief, but suddenly our evaluation of the man changes; in the area of politics beliefs are important!

Do Our Beliefs Matter?

In the realm of medicine the beliefs of a person often make the difference between life and death. Early in the 19th Century, a yellow fever epidemic broke out in New Orleans. The authorities believed that a brass band would bring a cure by disturbing the atmosphere. "The band paraded and pounded, the atmosphere was thoroughly disturbed, but the yellow fever was not." Because the medical beliefs were incorrect, the treatment failed and many people died.

We get another example of false medical beliefs from this report of the last days of Charles I of England:

"A pint of blood was extracted from the royal right arm, and a half pint from the royal left shoulder, followed by an emtic. The royal head was then shaven and a blister raised, then a sneezing powder, and a plaster of pitch on his feet. Finally, forty drops of extract of human skull were given— after which His Majesty gave up the ghost."

Of course he gave up the ghost! When medical beliefs are wrong, people's lives are endangered. Wrong medical beliefs still do untold harm in some of the remote areas of the world. When a young child in an isolated province of India becomes sick with a fever, the parents will often build a fire, heat up a piece of metal until it is white hot, and apply it to the hand of the child they love in the belief that this will scare away the demon of pain. The painful, searing heat, however, only adds to the child's misery. It is a medical tragedy when people hold the wrong beliefs.

In the matter of family life, we find that beliefs are most important. A girl's parents are talking about her plans to marry a very handsome young man. He seems to have all the qualifications a girl might want in a husband. He has a good education, a good job, a pleasing personality. There is only one catch. He views marriage as a temporary arrangement. He has been known to say: "I don't go for all this 'for better, for worse; in sickness and in health' bit. As long as we are happy together, as long as we are having a good time, and there are no arguments, we'll remain married. But, when the sparks begin to fly, we'll each find a new partner." In spite of his obvious qualifications, the young man's beliefs would probably destroy his forthcoming marriage.

In every area of life we find that our beliefs are crucially important. Right beliefs usually lead to success, joy, and health. False beliefs frequently lead to failure, sadness, ill health, or tragedy. This is no less true of our religious convictions than of our other ideas. The philosophy of life a person adheres to, the theology one holds, the values one prizes, these are the things that determine the kind of life one leads.

Bad ethical beliefs and theological concepts are disastrous. Adolph Hitler had his beliefs. He said that conscience was just an archaic Jewish invention. That spelled out his ethics! Over the gateway to the Buchenwald Concentration Camp the Nazi theology was stated in one short sentence; "There is no God here." This moral and theological vacuum was filled with the philosophy of the Master Race. Acting on the Nazi belief, Hitler's armies invaded Germany's peaceful neighbors until the quiet countryside of Europe was scarred with the horror of war. The Nazi creed led inexorably to the Nazi deed.

In similar manner, the Communist creed leads to the Communist deed. One of the key operational ideas of Communism is that it doesn't matter what means are employed as long as the end in view is worthwhile. Lenin said: "We must be ready to employ trickery, deceit, lawbreaking, withholding and concealing truth, in our efforts to build a better world." Under Communism vast populations were exterminated; whole countries have been made into concentration camps. In the realm of morals beliefs are of the utmost importance.

Do Our Beliefs Matter?

Our religious beliefs are important too, in that they give us a certain joyous zest in life. If we have a joyous philosophy that is grounded in reality, then our lives will be joyous and radiant. Victor stated the case well in Maxwell Anderson's "Key Largo": "I have to believe there's something in the world that isn't evil—I have to believe there's something in the world that would rather die than accept injustice—something positive for good—that can't be destroyed—or I'll die inside."

Many of the atheistic thinkers have a grim creed that saps the spirit of joy from their lives. Jean Paul Sartre says in "The Philosophy of the Absurd": "Man is alone, abandoned on earth in the midst of his infinite responsibility, without hope, with no other aims than the ones he sets for himself, with no other destiny than the one he forges for himself on this earth...All conduct will always be absurd in an absurd world."

Sartre's conclusion is that "life is absurd, love is impossible...all life is ambiguous."

Imagine rising from sleep in the morning, stretching, and then reverently saying to yourself: "Life is absurd; love is impossible; I am abandoned here on earth in the midst of infinite responsibilities." How could you experience joy as you faced your daily tasks with this philosophy?

The novelist, Theodore Dreiser, had filled his mind with the husks of skepticism. Near the end of his life, he wrote: "I go from this world, as I came into it, knowing nothing but confusion and dismay."

Clarence Darrow, the famed lawyer, filled his mind with the thoughts of atheism. In his later years he said of his life: "If I had it to do over again, I'd chuck it all." In his thinking suicide was preferable to life.

Many of us have missed the joy and radiance of life—the wonderful zest that comes from dynamic Christian believing and living. Thoreau noticed that the mass of humankind live "lives of quiet desperation." Perhaps that is the affliction you have experienced. Could it be that we do not believe fervently enough? It was not a clergyman, but one of the world's most noted psychotherapists, Carl Jung, who thought back on the case histories of the people who had come to him and said that lack of religion was the root of his patients' problems.

"Among all my patients in the second half of life—that is to say, over thirty-five—there has not been one whose problems in the last resort were not that of finding a religious outlook on life. It is safe to say that everyone of them fell ill because he had lost that which the living religions of every age have given to their followers, and none of them has been really healed who did not regain his religious outlook."

A sound religious value system is a necessity if we are to experience the truly abundant life.

Does it matter what we believe? In every phase of life it is crucially important. It is certainly true that our deep seated religious convictions determine our destiny more than we imagine. "As a man thinketh in his heart, so is he."

Chapter 2

Christianity

Of all the religious narratives in the world none is more beautiful than that which begins: "Now when Jesus was born in Bethlehem of Judea..." (Matthew 2:1)

Of all the spiritual teachings that have been presented through heaven's holy men, none are more sublime than those that say, "Blessed are the poor in spirit, for theirs is the kingdom of heaven." (Matthew 5:3)

Of all the prayers that prophets prayed and all the love that they shared, no prayer has ever brought the nature of God nearer or made it clearer than the prayer that begins, "Our Father who art in heaven..." (Matthew 6:9)

Of all the evidences of the power and glory of messiahship to which the world's scriptures testify, none lives deeper in the souls of people than the report, "You are the Christ, the Son of the living God." (Matthew 16:16)

Of all the promises that the scriptures of humankind hold out to us, of all the gospels of good news and hope with which the world is filled, no promise rings with greater hope than the words, "Because I live, you will live also... (John 14:19)

Some of us have been privileged to visit the scenes where we could relive the Christian story. As you stand in the Shepherds' Field and crowd into the Shepherds' Cave near Bethlehem you imagine that you hear the angels' song. For Christianity is a sentimental faith—a simple, believing, trusting faith.

In the Church of the Nativity you bow in reverence before the star marked manger, realizing more than ever that Christianity has not left unsatisfied the universal human desire to worship or the wish to probe the mysteries of the supernatural.

In Nazareth you drink from the well that you know was the one from which Mary drew water for her family; and you look down the street and say 'Perhaps it was here that Jesus worked. Here is where the carpenter shop may have stood.' Christianity more than any other faith is conscious of the close relationship of work and worship.

Beside the Sea of Galilee I imagined I heard him say, "Follow me, and I will make you fishers of men." (Matthew 4:19) For the religion of Christ is a religion of vocation.

In Bethany where he loved to visit, like every other Christian traveller we were escorted down into a tomb some twenty feet within the earth. Perhaps it was here, outside this silent grave, that he stood and called in a loud voice, "Lazarus, come out." (John 11:43) Christianity has always insisted that death does not ultimately have the last word. Death is an enemy to be overcome, a mystery to be solved, a victory to be won.

We went to "dark Gethsemane" where olive trees, reminiscent of his loneliness, stand in the hallowed garden. Nearby, inside a church, we found enshrined the stone on which it is said he prayed that night. Like every other person who loves his faith Evelyn and I knelt there, believing that Christianity in a very special way has found and revealed the creative power of prayer.

We walked the Via Dolorosa, the way of sorrow. There are always those who follow this winding path, and pray at the stations. There are always those who pause reverently and silently, and reflective, they remember his example and are ashamed of their uncommitted lives.

And then we went to Golgatha. There are two places called Golgatha in Jerusalem, and you may take your choice or visit both of them as we did. One elaborately sanctified, is

Christianity

found inside the present city; the other a gaunt and lonely hill resembling a skull, is outside the ancient walls.

As we stood in the shadow of that hill, with our eyes toward Jerusalem the vision of Christianity was clear. It is that this is the religion of the revelation of God in Jesus Christ, and were it not for him, it would be just another faith.

From Golgatha the Christian story unfolds as on a screen. You see the lowly Galilean as Son of God and Son of Man. You recognize him as the historical Jesus, working at his father's trade until the momentous day when he heard John the Baptist calling people to repent and proclaiming the coming of the Kingdom. When he comes to John to be baptized, Jesus has the wonderful assurance from the Father: "This is my beloved Son..." (Matthew 3:17) You see him as the living Christ, a divine reality working in the world today. Brought into the world and pervading it by the grace of God, he is sustained in the world by his mystical Body, which is the Church of true believers.

From Golgatha you see him through the teaching of your faith and through your vision, wisdom, hope, and inner longing, and that is why he is seen differently by different individuals. He came to fulfill the Law. For some he was a Jew who never travelled very far from the Jewish faith. To others he was a revolutionist against Judaism. To still others he was the Exemplary Man. To those who really knew him in the New Testament sense he was God incarnate.

You see it all from Golgatha. You see Christianity with its variegated followers—1,700,000,000—the largest among all the religions of the world. You see its more than a quarter of a million churches in the United States and its more than 200 denominational expressions. You see its schools, hospitals, homes, its great cathedrals, its lowly missions, its city chapels and its wayside shrines. You see it in Rome and Moscow, in peace and war, in joy and in sorrow. Wherever and whenever humans highest relationship with

This I Believe

God is contemplated, there Christianity is found. Christianity is the religion of the revelation of God in Christ.

Christ was different and distinctive among prophets and religious teachers. He spoke with authority unlike that of any man. The Fatherhood of God showed forth in him. The brotherhood of man was revealed in him. He taught the meaning of sin, repentance and forgiveness. He demonstrated neighborliness and non-resistance. He revealed the deepest insights into rewards and punishments. He brought a noble, persuasive gospel, using a child as an illustration of faith, a shepherd as a symbol of love, and a lowly Samaritan as an example of selfless service.

He had prophecies for those who benefitted from them, signs for those who wanted them, and miracles for those who needed them. But for those who caught the glory of his presence, there was always the challenge to higher living and greater trust in God.

Looking down into Jerusalem from the Mount of Olives, facing the Golden Gate, you can imagine what our Savior's triumphal march into the Temple Area on that first Palm Sunday was like. You will remember the Feast of the Passover, the plot against him, the betrayal, arrest, trial, the release of Barabbas, and the Crucifixion by the Romans on the hill where criminals were ignominiously put to death. It was here on Golgatha that his cross was lifted up. It was here, probably that he looked out upon the world and up into the heart of God; it was here that he spoke the seven last words.

Throughout the hundreds of years that have passed since darkness fell over the city at the death of God's Annointed One, interpreters have been trying to define exactly what Christianity is, what it implies, and how it stands in relationship to other religions of the world. Theologians have labeled it a revealed religion, a religion of regeneration and redemption, an experiential religion, a religion of Logos, a faith of doctrine and deed.

From strictest orthodoxy to liberal humanism, from the coming of the Kingdom by an instantaneous miracle to its evolvement through struggle and growth, from evangelistic stress upon self-denial to the modern emphasis upon self-realization, Christianity has many expressions. But in every case, in every school of thought, in every sectarian camp, Christianity is the religion of the revelation of God in Christ. And it does not speak of a Christ whose life and teachings were snuffed out on a hangman's hill.

For the most part this faith was founded not on the happenings of Golgatha, but on what took place in a garden only a few hours later. There the sorrowing women who had come to anoint the dead body of their beloved Master found instead an empty tomb.

We must leave Golgatha, and go now to the garden. Some call it the garden tomb, others the garden of Joseph of Arimathea. It is a quiet, sequestered spot with flowers, a well, and an empty sepulchre. It qualifies well for Christendom's remembrance of the first hallowed Easter morn. "He is not here," the Scripture says, "for he has risen, as he said." (Matthew 28:6)

Here from the garden of the Resurrection you can look out across the Christian Era, and you can see the full sweep of Christianity in a new perspective. You realize that with all its divisions, factions, diversities it is actually more united than we realize. It is united in the risen Christ, and, because of this, the likenesses of these groups outweigh their differences. The miracle of the garden is that all denominations and all expressions of Christianity can be assembled here, and still there is room.

There is room for the disciples from Thomas, the doubter, to impetuous Peter. Paul, the first great missionary, is here, and all the saints and martyrs of the early church are present. The followers of Christ—called "Christians" first at Antioch and recognized by their love for one another—they are here. Those who preserved the early letters of the Church—the Church Fathers—they are here also.

Walking in the garden, I felt that the so called heretics—those who opposed the fixed dogmas of the institutionalized church—were also here. For history does not deny the fact that Christianity frequently became involved in a struggle for power—political power, state power, and world power. All such problems were far from the intention of Jesus Christ and were greatly opposed to the simple teachings that he had proclaimed. Always there have been those who saw Christianity as God's sword to conquer the 'heathen'. Constantine the Great claimed that on his way to Rome at the head of his warring troops he saw, as in a vision, a flaming cross against the sky. And over the cross he saw the words, "In this sign conquer."

Christianity became the state religion of the Roman Empire, and the Church grew. Indeed, there were centuries in which it was known as the Holy Catholic Church and emperors were crowned and dethroned, "holy wars" were encouraged, and crusades were instigated. The idea was to "save" Christianity from pagan threats, and even to convert the "heathen," to capture Jerusalem, and also to find the cup from which Christ drank at his Passover Feast with his disciples—The Holy Grail.

As time went on the vaunted Holy Catholic Church was torn by schism and hatreds and struggles for power. In the East the mighty Byzantine Empire claimed Jesus to be the founder of its faith no less than did the Catholic Church of Rome. The latter insisted that it had primacy to the claim of the one true Church and that its pope was God's chosen vicar of Christ. The patriarch of eastern Catholicism disagreed and in 1054 ex-communicated the pope of Rome, who had already sought to excommunicate the patriarch.

So what was called the one true Church became two churches, and all through the ensuing years there were followers of Christ outside the formidable walls of both these lavish kingdoms of the lowly Nazarene. Groups like the Moravian Brethern, the Waldenses, and the Anabaptists said they, too, belonged to the true Church. Individuals of deep commitment like John Huss, John Wycliffe, Girolamo Savonarola, and Gerhard Groote were convinced that God had given them revelations too. And there was room for all of them in the garden of the resurrected Christ.

The reformers were in the garden too—men who wrote one of the most thrilling chapters in the march of the Christian faith. Martin Luther, the Augustinian monk was here, challenging Roman Catholicism to define and justify its doctrines and examine its conduct in the light of scriptural truth; John Calvin, John Knox, Huldreich Zwingli, and other reformers were all within the growing ranks of Protestantism. Protestantism—which had nothing to protest and everything to proclaim—became the passionate expression of a people's faith and, it was believed, the reinstatement of the teachings of Christ.

There in the Garden I could understand how Protestantism, born in schism, continued to be schismatic. Created by the impulse of reform, it has followed reform tactics down through the years. It was determined to rediscover the Christ and recapture his spirit, and the rediscovery was to be continual.

One man served as an excellent example of the best and most impressive post-Reformation advocates for a purer, holier, and more consecrated life. John Wesley dominated 18th century Protestantism both in personal dedication and in the evangelistic revival, urging and inspiring people to believe in the changeless gospel of Christ. He was a graduate of Oxford, a fellow of Lincoln College, a lin-

This I Believe

guist, a minister, and missionary; but he was first of all a dedicated man of deep commitment.

With his brother Charles, poet and writer of six thousand gospel hymns, John Wesley put into practice the principles inherent in Christ's teaching and life. By a rigid devotion to what they thought of as spiritual habits they generated a power and so inspired others to follow their example that the world nick-named them "Methodists" because of their methodical devotion. From such a beginning and by means of the contagion of the triumphant Christian spirit the Methodist denomination came into existence. The fellowship of the United Methodist Church today in America alone includes over nine million persons.

In the Garden of the Resurrection we can visualize the cavalcade of the various representatives of the Christian faiths passing in review at the open tomb: members of the Eastern Orthodox Church, Roman Catholics, Copts, silent Quakers, shouting Pentecostals, and Unitarians. 'Who can count the members of the Christian world or estimate their potential? Whoever and wherever they are, whatever they believe and teach and seek to live, they are all part of the heritage of faith which claims a risen Lord,

No other religion presents the claim or proves the claim that Christianity has made to the world. No other scripture leads men and women away from the garden tomb as confidently and as beautifully as does the Christian story: "Then he led them out as far as Bethany, and lifting up his hands, he blessed them." (Luke 24:50-51) "And while they were gazing into heaven as he went, behold two men stood by them in white robes, and said, 'Men of Galilee, why do you stand looking into heaven? This Jesus who was taken up from you into heaven, will come in the same way as you saw him go into heaven." (Acts 1:10-11)

This too, is the Christian hope—that Jesus Christ will come again. And this also is interpreted in countless ways

Christianity

by the 1,700,000,000. citizens of Christendom. Their views are many, their opinions are varied and strongly individualized. But in the deepest spirit of their quest there is a basic, irrevocable agreement. A united conviction is expressed in a universally accepted and dearly loved text that every Christian knows, respects, and believes…"For God so loved the world that he gave his only Son, that whoever believes in him should not perish but have eternal life." (John 3:16)

Christianity is the religion of the revelation of God in Christ.

This I Believe

Chapter 3

How To Find God

I came across a clipping I had cut out of the paper some time ago. It told about a diver who had brought up a seven foot, ten and a half pound, gold chain, representing part of the treasure they had found on a Spanish Galleon which broke apart in a hurricane in 1622. It reminded me of a parable I had heard.

Once upon a time a fabulous fortune was lost at sea. Three men heard about it; and each desired to possess the treasure and spend the rest of his days in peace.

The first man decided that he would wait until he really needed the money before going in search of it. "Time enough to worry about that," he said, "when I'm in a jam."

The second man, on the contrary, couldn't get started soon enough; and hiring the first craft he came upon he set out on his own, without bothering to get any further particulars or help. He spent the rest of his life searching for the treasure but to no avail. Tossed about on the stormy seas he didn't know where to begin looking, nor where to turn for shelter.

The third man, however, inquired as to the general location of the treasure; secured the necessary charts and tools; set out in search; and found the treasure.

All of us desire to possess that great spiritual treasure which awaits those who find God. Job voiced the universal desire of humankind when he cried out: "O that I knew where I might find him!" Is God to blame for our dilemma? Has he hidden himself so well that only the fortunate few ever find him? Oh no, the trouble lies with us. We have been either like the first man who decided to put off the search until he was in a jam (witness the countless number

This I Believe

of people who seek out a clergy person when they are in trouble); or we have been like the second man who floundered about on the storm tossed seas because he did not know where to look.

In this great game of Hide and Seek, the trouble has been that either we have been "base stickers," or we have wandered around pretending to search but really waiting for God to show himself.

"Seek and you shall find," we have been promised. So let us concern ourselves with the chart and the tools for the search.

Thomas Carlyle once said that Nature is the garment of God; and if we look closely enough at God's garment, we may find God himself. And yet, how many of us miss this glorious revelation. We are too much occupied with other things to take time to look at Nature. We often pity people who live in crowded cities because they cannot see the beauty of nature; but even those who live in beautiful suburbs or countrysides often fail to catch glimpses of God's glorious garments. Ask yourself, as you look at the beauty all around you, are you feeling the power of God's presence, or are you too busy to bother? Are we saying to ourselves, "Some day, when there isn't so much to worry about I shall take time to look for God in Nature?" If we belong with the busy people, perhaps we had better be careful. Each changing scene in the drama of the Seasons offers new opportunities, it is true; but who knows that for you and for me the chance may not come again! Spring may come, but we may not see it. Autumn may come, and we may not be here. It is better to look for God today.

"Oh I can hear you, God, above the cry of the tossing trees
Rolling your windy tides across the sky
And splashing your silver seas
Over the pine,

*To the water line
Of the moon. Oh I can hear you God,
Above the wail of the lonely loon
When the pine tops pitch and nod
Chanting their melodies
Of ghostly waterfalls and avalanches,
Swishing your wind among the branches,
To make them pure and white.
Wash over me God, with your piney breeze,
And your moon's wet silver pool.
Wash over me God, with your wind and night,
And leave me clean and cool."*

Yes, it is better to find God in Nature today!

But God does not confine himself to the garments of Nature. He can be found too in the robes of Knowledge. We are all seekers after knowledge. We belong to an age that is driven ahead by its intense desire for knowledge. There never was a time when education was so general. Our great institutions of learning are daily unravelling some secret of the universe, and the discoveries of our seekers after knowledge are revolutionizing the world. But within this great panorama of knowledge which is daily spreading itself before us do we hear God speaking? Are we finding God? God is the core of all knowledge, the hidden source of all truth; and no matter how much we learn, if we do not find God at the source, we have learned nothing of lasting value.

It is doubtful if we, as a generation, have been searching deeply enough into knowledge to find God. Oh, we have been proud of our discoveries, but we have not yet learned how to relate our discoveries to the love of God.

There is a well known story about the man who thought he knew so much that he could make a man, He did know a great deal, and the story has it that he actually made the body of a man; but without God, he could not give the man a soul. He could not give him that spirit-thing called reason which is man's crowning glory; so the man that he made became a monster who turned upon his maker and rent him to pieces.

As a generation, we have gained enough knowledge only to make a monster, that has turned upon us to rend us to pieces.

Take one simple illustration that might pass for a parable: somewhere in a university town in this country there lives a brilliant research chemist. I don't know his name or a single thing about him, but I would make an inspired guess that he is a decent, kindly man, because most people are. It was his technical virtuosity which made possible the addition of an extra ingredient to napalm so that the burning jelly would stick with greater tenacity to human skin, defying the efforts of its victims or doctors to scrape it off until it had done its disfiguring work.

No doubt, every morning before that brilliant man set off for his laboratory, he would fondly kiss the skin of his children without making any conscious mental connection between that simple fatherly act and the complex chemistry in which he was totally absorbed—otherwise he would have gone stark, raving mad.

Yes, we have found in Knowledge the formulae for our chemicals, the designs for our great machines, the secret of the atom; but we have not found God. So our chemicals designed for our good, become weapons with which to kill; and our machines, built to free us from slavery, become the monstrous instruments of our utter enslavement. In our quest for Knowledge, if we will look for God at its source, we will find Him. Then we shall know the Truth, and the Truth shall set us free.

God speaks to us through Nature and Knowledge, but he also has a way of coming to us in Opportunity. Opportunity comes to each of us daily, and many times God

How To Find God

comes with it. Sometimes we see Him, but many times we neither see God nor the opportunity until both have gone by and passed on. How much interest do we show in our friends, in our families, in our neighbors, and in the stranger who finds his way to our gates? Do we recognize need when it stands upon our threshold? Do we look for God as he passes by in the opportunity to help others, or are we all wrapped up in our own troubles?

There was an old shoemaker named Martin. He was a poor man, and lived in a little shop in a dingy street; but he was a lover of God and a lover of people. One night, in a dream he heard a voice, and the voice said to him, "Martin, I am the Lord whom you love. Tomorrow look well in the streets, for I am coming by."

In the morning old Martin awoke and tidied up his little shop, making it neat and clean for the eyes of his Lord. Then he sat down at his bench by the window, and went to work. But he could not keep his eyes on the shoe that he was mending, for he kept thinking that, at any moment, the Lord might walk past his window and pause at the door.

However, the morning passed, and he saw no one but an old man shoveling snow. He watched the poor old man slap his hands against his body to put warmth in them. Alas, thought Martin, the poor old man is freezing from the bitter cold. Perhaps while I am waiting for the Lord to come by, I could make him a cup of tea. So he made a cup of tea and took it to the old man who drank gratefully of its steaming warmth. And carrying the old man's warm words of thanks, Martin went back to his shop and his bench, and took up his vigil once again.

The day wore on, and still he did not see the Lord. Then he saw the thin form of a woman as she came down the street, vainly struggling with a ragged old shawl to protect her child from the bitter wind. Martin's tender heart was touched by the tragic look on her face; so, as she passed his window, he knocked gently on the glass to attract her attention, and beckoned her to come in. Gladly she came to the warmth of his stove, and gratefully accepted his gentle offer of food and a warm coat of his own with which to wrap the child.

For an hour or so, the woman and her child lingered in the cozy warmth of Martin's little shop; and then they were gone, leaving behind their heartfelt thanks. Martin again sat down at the bench by the window, but now he could scarcely see. The street was now dark. His eyes were old, and he could no longer see the form of any who might pass his window. The day had passed, and the Lord had not come. Sadly he laid aside his tools, lighted the lamp, and sat down by the glowing stove to read his Bible. In the warmth and the silence he soon fell asleep, and in his sleep he heard the Voice again. And the voice said, "Martin, did you know me when I came?" Martin stirred, and said, "But Lord, you did not come. How could I know you?"

And the Voice answered, "Yes, but I did come this day, for this was I." And there passed before Martin the figure of the old man who had shoveled the snow. Then he saw the woman and the child, and the Voice said, "This was I."

The Vision passed, and the Voice was silent. Then Martin awoke, his gaze falling on the page of the open Bible upon his lap, and there he read these words: "For I was hungry, and you gave me meat; I was thirsty, and you gave me drink; I was a stranger, and you took me in; naked and you clothed me. Verily, I say unto you, inasmuch as you have done it unto one of the least of these my brethern, you have done it unto me."

Martin had truly found God, because he had seen the need of others and had taken the opportunity to help them. There is need for people like Martin in the kind of world we live in. Let us remember that the power of Christianity lies in its selflessness. And let us be careful that we do not become so engrossed in ourselves and our own problems that we have no time for others. May we never miss the chance to find God in the opportunities to help others.

So we find God in the garments of Nature, the robes of Knowledge, and in Opportunity; but God may be found in yet a greater and clearer form—in the form of the man, Jesus.

When Philip turned to Jesus and said: "Lord, show us the Father and we shall be satisfied." Jesus replied: "Philip, he who has seen me has seen the Father. If you would know what God is like, if you would understand the power behind all things. then take a long look at me."

I turn the pages of the Gospel and look at the record that we have of the life and ministry of Jesus Christ. I see his healing ministry. I see the way in which he dealt with individual men and women. I see the tenderness with which he handled the sins and miseries of people. I see the purity of his life. I listen to him speak and I catch the accents of compassion in his words. My heart begins to warm with his tremendous and thrilling affirmation. What we are seeing on the stage of history as we look at Jesus and listen to Jesus is the eternal God revealing himself. "Jesus thou art all compassion, pure unbounded love thou art!" That is God writing his own autobiography. That is the God who stands behind all things. "He who has seen me," said Jesus, "has seen the Father."

I read an interesting interview one time which had been given by Alec Guiness, the famous movie actor. Guiness, a devoted Christian and a devout Roman Catholic, told the interviewer how it was that he became a Christian and a Catholic. For some years he was an agnostic, and he had the typical approach to life of an agnostic. He believed that life was a matter of chance and there was no power behind things at all. One time he was playing the lead in the filming of the Father Brown stories written by G. K. Chesterton. They were filming on location in a little village in France.

One night, when the filming was finished, Guiness began to walk home to the village where he was staying. He was still wearing the priest's garb that he wore in the film. It was a very dark night, and as he began to walk along the village lane, he heard footsteps running behind him. It was a little French boy who came up to him and held his hand tightly and walked through the darkness with him to the village, chattering happily all the way. Guiness kept absolutely quiet. He did not dare to speak, lest his accent frighten the boy, and the boy would realize that he was not a bona fide Catholic priest, although he was dressed like one.

He kept absolutely quiet. When they got to the village, the boy unloosed his hand giving it one final squeeze, and went happily into his own house. Guiness said that he stopped there in the village square and began to think. That boy trusted him because he wore the uniform of something that represented trust to him. He believed that he was his father in God and trusted his life in his hands. Surely, Guiness thought, there is a greater Father, and I can trust my life in his hands. From that little incident, he became a man who trusted his life into the hands of the God who had been revealed as his father in Jesus Christ. "He who has seen me has seen the Father." This is the character of the God with whom we have to deal, a God who loves us, each one, as though there were but one to love.

For thirty-three years God walked and talked with people in the person of Jesus of Nazareth, but only a few recognized that he was God. The others nailed him to a cross. So great was their blindness! But the blindness did not stop with the cross on Golgatha's hill. Each generation nails him up anew. The same old blindness strikes us all; the blindness of self. We cannot find God in Christ, or in anything else, because we are oblivious to everything but ourselves. Our hearts and minds must be emptied of the world before we can see God. And how do we do it? Only by giving ourselves, body, soul, mind and spirit to the cause of Christ. His Kingdom must become the most important thing in our lives. We must become spiritually minded instead of materially minded. When we look at the world with spiritual and not material values in mind, we begin to see things that we have never seen before. We begin to find God in everything that touches our daily lives. Instead of groping for God in the darkness, never seeing him, never finding him, through Jesus we seek and find him in all beauty, knowledge, and opportunity, remembering that Jesus said: "Seek and you shall find; knock and the door will be opened."

In our search for God, however, there is one trap we must be careful not to fall into. The Old Testament states that God made man in his own image. Yet, far too often we each attempt to make God in our image. How easily and uncritically we believe that God likes what we like, approves of what we approve, hates what we hate, believes in and supports the same values as we do, has the same prejudices and blind spots as we do. Sometimes we even go so far as to believe that God belongs to the same political party and religious denomination as we do.

The Old and New Testaments make it plain that humans cannot alter God. To attempt to do this is to stray from the truth. It seems wise for us occasionally to ask what type of God we want and to consider if the god we want is actually the God that is. Stop and consider whether you have been attempting to make God in your own image.

The type of God many are seeking today is a cosmic Santa Claus. They want Him to protect their privileged position, their wealth, health and comfort; and to approve of their selfishness. He is to be on their side, to be their God in the sense that they own Him. In fact, He is valid to them only as He supports their race, ecclesiastical organization, political and economic point of view.

I do not mean to imply by this that God disagrees or disapproves of all that such persons think and do. Undoubtedly many of their ideas coincide with God's truths. The point is that they do not seek first God's Kingdom or righteousness. They attempt to make God approve of what they do and think, rather than first learning what God approves of and then ordering their lives accordingly. Theirs is not real faith. It is not betting their lives on love, justice and truth. It is not fighting evil. It is not seeking to pattern their lives according to God's will. Their God makes no demands on them, they make them of him. They give the orders, but take none themselves.

But God is not made in our image. Any such attempt is doomed to failure. We can in no way alter or change truth. We can only discover it. Valid faith seeks God's judgement. It does not seek to make God in one's own image, but to be made in God's image.

Of course, in our quest for God we are never fully satisfied. We all yearn to know exactly what God is like. If God is infinite, if He is beyond all we can completely understand, then we will never know God in His entirety. We can have some intimations of His nature, but essentially God will remain a mystery. This is what the writer of Hebrews pointed toward when he both asked and answered: "And what is faith? Faith gives substance to our hopes, and makes us certain of realities we do not see."

To have faith is to bet one's life on that which cannot be ultimately proved. Faith leaps beyond proof and sight. It takes up where reason leaves off. It isn't unreasonable. It only acts on what seems reasonable, but is ultimately unprovable.

You may say: "But I cannot worship and believe in a God who is all mystery." Let me hasten to add that God isn't all mystery. The New Testament makes plain that He revealed something of Himself in Jesus called the Christ.

There is ample evidence about God for the person who truly wants to believe.

Dean Miller once said that we can believe in God if it is really God we want to believe in. But if all we want is a divine protector of our privileges and prejudices, a surefire refuge against every consequence of our own stupidity and malice, a convenient means of getting out of every dire emergency—then we are not acting on faith at all, but on superstition.

When we realize that we cannot put limits around God, we can never completely know him, that he is infinite, then our faith responds, and we know Him best of all. Many never have a vital faith because their God is too small. The Judeo-Christian God is one before whom we must stand in awe; a God capable of being worshiped. When we believe we have completely described God in theological statements, creeds or dogmas, we have actually shut God out as He can never be completely enclosed in finite concepts or descriptions. Even when we have said all we can about God, He essentially remains a mystery, an unknown.

In the final analysis, faith is a venture into an unknown land. It is betting one's life on the God who is essentially mystery, but who revealed enough of Himself in Jesus the Christ to make evident that He exists, that His basic nature is love, and that He is constantly working to bring the triumph of goodness and the destruction of evil. When the writer of Hebrews talks about faith, he says it is a venture into new territory on the basis of trust in realities that are not seen.

Our faith is weak today because we do not do this. We play it safe. We want proof. All the evidence must be in before we will act. We are afraid to exercise our imaginations, to try the unpopular, to attempt the untried, to do that which might cost us something, which might threaten our privileged position, our comfort, and our power.

When the author of Hebrews says: "By faith we perceive that the universe was fashioned by the word of God, so that the visible came forth from the invisible," he described a condition that continues to take place.

As a very young boy I used to think that the waving of the branches caused the wind. Why not? Whenever the branches wave the wind blows; the wind never does blow except when the branches wave. Is not that the simplest explanation to account for the invisible by the movements of the visible? But believe it or not, the invisible wind comes first; even in the physical world the great causations come from the unseen.

Creation has not ended. The universe continues to be fashioned by the word of God, by God's creative power and truth.

God continues today to bring forth the visible from the invisible. An evil thought leads to an evil action. The good thought leads to good action. Faith which is invisible, produces words and deeds that are visible. A lack of faith brings futility and inaction.

It may seem of little importance what we believe about God, but living in accordance with the truth or against it makes a tremendous difference. Our own lives and the life of our nation will wither like the grass in the field unless they are built on God's truth. It is important, therefore, that we not attempt to make God in our own image, but to allow our lives to be molded according to God's image of truth, justice and love. If our desire is truly to seek His Kingdom and His righteousness, we will live by faith that is an adventure, a faith that rests on and responds to the mystery of God.

Faith is more than belief. Mere belief may become a sterile, lifeless thing. A creed by itself may degenerate into insincere pious talk. Faith is a belief plus a venture. It is a creed in action. It is the commitment of one's all to God in whom you believe. So Paul, writing of the faith that strengthened him for every task, which supported him as he was about to pass through the gates of death, says, "I know whom I have believed, and am persuaded that he is able to keep that which I have committed unto him against that day." (II Timothy 1:12 K.J.)

Herein lies the chief cause of our spiritual blindness. It is not so much on account of our unbelief that we fail in our quest for God, as our failure to commit ourselves to what we actually believe. Faith is belief plus decision and action.

Christopher Columbus believed that the earth was round, and that on an uncharted sea he might find his way to the other side of the globe. He set out on the great adventure. Mysteries and storms engulfed him. Doubts and fears seized the hearts of the men who were with him. They counseled that they turn back as voices in the soul sometimes urge us to turn back from our quest for God and rest lazily in our unbelief. But the intrepid commander answered, "Sail on! Sail on!" Then came the day when on the horizon land appeared, and they set their feet upon a shore more beautiful and plentiful than their fondest dreams. Here is belief, and a venture, and realization!

We who venture on our belief in God will find our fairest hopes confirmed. Belief in God, commitment to Him, assurance of Him and by Him—this is the faith that overcomes the world. This is the key that unlocks God's treasures of grace—the conviction that undergirds all life with confidence and high expectation—the gleam that lights our pilgrim way until we come at last to the City of God.

This I Believe

Chapter 4

The Uniqueness of Jesus

In a little book entitled, "Christianity Among the Religions of the World," Arnold Toynbee, the historian, calls on Christian people to purge our Christianity of its exclusiveness. That is, the traditional belief that Christianity is unique. According to Toynbee this insistence of ours on the uniqueness of Christ is a subtle form of pride, and it stands in the way of unity with other religions in our common struggle against atheism and godlessness. Get rid of this dogma, advises Toynbee.

Well, as the circus performer once said, "It would be a good trick if we could do it." The uniqueness of Christ is deeply embedded in our consciousness. It is what gives us our Gospel. We find something more in Christ than in any other; something original, sublime, transcendent in his words and deeds that mark him and make a difference. "Never a man spake as this man." "None other name…"

However, as Toynbee has said the time has come when we need to re-examine our belief in the uniqueness of Christ, but not so we can get rid of this belief. Rather in order that we might know what we mean when we assert it.

The world we live in now is not as compartmentalized as it once was where each nation or religion could live behind protective walls, safe from the invasion of others. We are being increasingly exposed to new contacts with old religions. There is no fence high enough to keep out alien ideas. The smoldering fires of some of the old religions are being fanned by the winds of nationalism. There is a revival going on in the non-Christian religions. They're becoming missionary, aggressive.

Furthermore, simultaneous with this invasion of non-Christian ideas, there has been a radical change in the attitude of Christians toward other faiths. A generation ago our mission studies focused attention mainly on the errors and evils to be found in these 'other' religions. We were inclined to compare our best with their worst. It's not easy for Christians to be objective. Then we remember what Jesus said about coming not to destroy but to fulfill.

So I say we need to re-examine our beliefs in the uniqueness of Christ, and I think we have to begin by getting clear in our minds what we mean by 'uniqueness'. In what does the originality of Jesus consist? If by originality we mean novelty, a teacher who comes with thoughts absolutely new, saying what was never said before, thinking thoughts no one before has ever taught, we misrepresent the facts. That just is not it. In fact, one clear law of the mind is that there is nothing absolutely original, no idea that is wholly, completely new. Even the airplane was put together out of something old, the combination of ideas and inventions which had passed through the minds of many men. Someone complimented Thomas Edison on his originality. "I am not original." he said, "I'm a good sponge. Most of my ideas come from others who didn't trouble to use them."

In music there seems an inexhaustible supply of melodies. Yet none of them are wholly new. I once heard that there had been a standing offer in Vienna of twenty-five thousand dollars to anyone who could write eight bars of original music, and that the offer has never been claimed. Many compositions have been submitted, but all of them have been traced back to some other melody.

So in the treasury of thought and the history of ideas, nothing is wholly new. "All literature," said Emerson, "is quotation." It is well known that Shakespeare was not original. He borrowed his plots from Plutarch's Lives, Danish folklore, and other sources. Lincoln made a speech at

The Uniqueness of Jesus

Gettysburg which his biographer tells us was written on the train. But, Herndon, his law partner, said that long before Mr. Lincoln went to the White House, he loaned him a book of sermons by Theodore Parker, and when the book was returned, one sentence was heavily underscored: "Democracy is self-government over all the people, for all the people, by all the people." And since then others have traced the words still further back to John Wycliffe in his "Preface to the Translation of the Bible." I say we need to be clear about this, so that we may go on to consider what we do mean by his uniqueness. In what does the originality of Christ consist?

Well first of all, put down his sublime simplicity. This may not be the most impressive, but neither is it unimportant. Part of his profound impact upon his contemporaries, and upon us, is due to the masterful way in which his clear mind simplified and clarified the great Law, the complexities and entanglements of thought. "You have heard it said, but I say…"

In the second century Christianity faced one of its cleverest and bitterest enemies, a Greek named Celsus. He despised this new superstition, Christianity, and with brilliant arguments he vigorously opposed it. And one of his most effective arguments among intellectuals was this one, that Jesus was a plagarist, that he borrowed his best utterances from other minds in the past. He was considerably non-plussed to discover that his Christian opponents seemed to have no disposition to dispute that. In fact, it has been pointed out over and over by Christian scholars that most of the teachings of Jesus can be paralleled elsewhere—in the prophets, the Psalms, the voluminous writings of the rabbis. This was the textbook of his boyhood. He made constant use of many ideas familiar in the rich religious heritage of his people.

This I Believe

The Kingdom of God was a concept long known and honored. He did not originate that. The idea of God as Father was certainly not new. The commandment: "Thou shalt love the Lord thy God with all thy heart and all thy soul," was a quotation from as far back as Deuteronomy. Even what we call "The Lord's Prayer" drew on little fragment expressions and aspirations of devout men long before. "The meek shall inherit the earth" is a quotation from the Thirty-seventh Psalm. "My God, why hast thou forsaken me?" is from the Twenty-second Psalm. "Father into thy hands I commend my spirit"—his last words from the cross was a common prayer. It was the "Now I lay me..." prayer of all Jewish children.

No, when we speak of the originality of Jesus we do not mean novelty. In his words are the voices of a thousand years. His uniqueness was in his emphasis, the unparalleled sublimity of his mind to see the difference between the true and the false, and to sift the essential from the trivial. The laws of his people were an immense entanglement. Even the best rabbis got lost in it—laws on top of laws, countless picayune rules. "A burden," he called it. "A burden grievous to be borne." "You have lost the Law of God." he said, "cluttered it up, made it have none effect by your traditions."

Where did he learn his wisdom? Who taught this Nazarene Carpenter, (who died, you remember, at thirty-three,) to see with penetrating clarity into the deep issues of life over which the scholars and rabbis had argued and wrestled? This is not the most impressive, but neither is it unimportant—the sublime clarity of his mind.

Another clear mark of his uniqueness is summed up in the word "fulfillment." He was born of a people prepared for thousands of years in a knowledge of God and a concept of human dignity unparalleled in any other race. His school was the synagogue. His textbook was the Law of the Prophets. For him the roots of faith went deep into the soil

The Uniqueness of Jesus

of his people's history. He saw God in all the great hopes of the past from which the best in the present had come. But while he accepted the past, he didn't stop with it. "I am come not to destroy, but to fulfill." He took up all the great insights of the past and fulfilled them, filled them full of larger, wider meaning. God! He took up the Old Testament vision of God. His people were the first monotheists—one God, but still a national God, the God of Israel, their God, the God of the nation—limited and local. He said when you pray, say "OUR Father," and all the fences in the world began to come down. The national became universal. "God so loved the world…" There was a whole new emphasis in that.

He took up the idea of the Kingdom of God. He didn't invent that, but he widened it, transformed it, cleaned it of its racial exclusiveness. "Seek it." he said, "seek it first. Make it the supreme loyalty of life." And so also, he took the great symbols of worship by which through centuries they had sought the presence of God—the Temple, the Altar, the Mercy Seat, the Feast Days. He did not disown them or destroy them, He fulfilled them, loosed them from their narrow, provincial limitations into wider universal meanings. "The Lord's Supper," for instance—the Passover Supper. It was intensely national. Every year it brought thousands of the devout to Jerusalem to celebrate the deliverance of the nation from the bondage of Egypt. It is still celebrated every year in one of the oldest ceremonies in history, and it exalts the idea of divine concern for one chosen people. Out of that nationalistic Passover Supper he made the Supper of Remembrance which has come to be the meeting place of millions from many, many races, cultures, and nations, exalting not the idea of God's concern for one people, but his sacrificial love for all people—the whole world. Everything he touched he lifted from the local to the universal, from the partial to the eternal. So that all the old ideas were filled with new meanings and larger universal light.

Furthermore, he gathered up the hopes and longings of lands and ages beyond his own. Scholarship today has furnished us with a wealth of new knowledge about old faiths, what we once called heathen religions. We know something now about the wisdom of the East. We have the sacred books of China, India, ancient Babylonia, old mythologies, mystery religions, some of them pretty terrible. Yet no religion is wholly false. Every religion, even the queerest, has some shining of a light. Why should that surprise us? It floors some people to learn that the Golden Rule is found in some fragmentary form in many faiths. Why should it surprise us that God has given light to other people? Pascal has said, "God has an infinite desire to communicate himself." And Christ will destroy no good thing in any faith. He will lift up every partial truth into larger universal light. "I am come not to destroy but to fulfill."

But we need to be very clear about this. There is an almost impassable gulf between Christ and the oriental faiths. It's all very well to discover parallels to his teachings, here and there some insights shared in common. But the fact remains that between the escape religions of the East that teach withdrawal from the world, and his vigorous call to change and transform the world, there is very little kinship. If one is true, the other isn't. If two and two make four, they never do make three. What these people who ask that we make common cause with old religions forget is that the blight which has fallen on much of the eastern world is caused by their religions. It is mostly why the Communists called religion "the opiate of the people." Escape religion has submerged the people's vital life in the peace and quietude of death. What they need, and what we need, is the touch of the transforming Christ. "I am come to fulfill." "I am come that you may have life, life that is more abundant."

But the highest word remains to be said. The clearest mark of his uniqueness is not in his words, but in him,

The Uniqueness of Jesus

summed up in the word "Incarnation"—the Word made flesh and brought to life in a Person. It is he himself who remains through the ages supreme and unparalleled. The words he spoke were not wholly new, but the Man was. "Never man spake as this man." Here is the supreme miracle of the ages—a Man who towers as high above our century as he did above the first. The world has made many great men. Their records are written in our histories. But who among them would you put along side of him? Where would you start?

There's a story about a Russian novelist who dreamed he stood in a crowded Russian Church. The standing congregation swayed in worship like grain before the wind. The sacred candles gleamed red against the altars. Suddenly in his dream he had a strong feeling that Christ was standing just behind him. He dared not turn, but he must; and turning he looked into his face. "What sort of Christ is this?" he thought. "Such an ordinary face. A face like all men's faces." And that is grandly true. The face that looks out from the Gospel pages is a human face, flesh of our flesh, bone of our bone—a face like all men's faces.

Through Jesus I came to know God. Christ lies at the very heart not only of my own individual religious experience, but of all Christianity, and it is only as we come to know the historic Jesus that we can fully comprehend the glory of our "Eternal Contemporary." The teachings of Jesus can best be understood when we realize they were presented by a human being with a very definite background, in a particular environment, with a specific historic setting. It gives added significance to the declarations of our Lord when we realize they are not mere theoretical solutions to hypothetical situations, but the Divine solution revealed to the Son who went through the human experience. "For we have not a high priest that cannot be touched with the feeling of our infirmities, but one that hath been in all points tempted like as we are, yet without sin."

Then too, as we come to know the historic Jesus we gain an intimate acquaintance with a very real person so that his very life becomes an example for us; and even where we have no record of his having dealt with problems analogous to some of ours we feel instinctively that we know what he would have done if he had. As I see Jesus, therefore, he was not a blueprint for life, but he offers an illustration of a life lived wholly in fidelity to the divine purpose, and may be used as a pattern for us in determining the divine purpose in our own very different problems.

Jesus can help us with our problems by serving as our authority in three ways. First, as our example in the way he dealt with perennial problems and universal experiences such as temptation and death. Secondly, in dealing with problems which are analogous to the ones which confronted Jesus we can imagine what Jesus would do in our situation. Finally, in problems where there is no real analogy he can help us as we get our spirits in tune with reality and seek solutions to our problems from the Living Christ.

Of the fact that there was an historical Jesus there can be no doubt, but when we attempt an accurate biography or portrait we find that our source material is, in reality, fragmentary. Nevertheless, by studying the fragments we have, we are able to get a very clear understanding of the Nazarene. The bulk of our material is to be found in the Synoptic Gospels, and fortunately for us these were written down during the lifetime of many who had witnessed the events recorded. Therefore, the Gospels had to be faithful to tradition, or they would have been rejected. This is evident when we realize that if the Evangelists had been following their own ends, they would have omitted instances which did not serve their end, and they would have filled in many gaps which now exist.

The Uniqueness of Jesus

While we look to the period of Jesus' ministry for our main information about him, in reality this covers only three years of his life, as compared to his infancy, boyhood, and young manhood. While the gospel record of the longer period of Jesus' life is but slight and not authenticated, nonetheless it does present a picture in harmony with the impressions left by the fuller and more reliable accounts. As I see Jesus, therefore, he was a child of a pious Jewish family. That such a one could have been born of a woman does indeed seem miraculous. Whether or not there was anything unnatural about his conception does not seem to me of fundamental importance however. While I would not categorically deny the Virgin Birth, neither would I unequivocally affirm it. Theirs was a mediocre family, the boy Jesus was one of several children, the father, a carpenter by trade, had to work hard and have the help of his sons in order to make a living. As the head of his household, Joseph saw to it that the whole family kept the Sabbath and attended the Synagogue worship. His children were educated in the Synagogue school and were steeped in the Law and the Prophets. The influence of his home and hometown on the boy Jesus must have been profound, for the rest of his life he remained a Nazarene. He also remained a Jew, although in this respect he was both a child of tradition and a rebel against tradition.

Jesus' concern for the poor takes on added significance when we realize how fully he understood their problem. Class division, economic oppression, minority persecutions…these are not new to our generation. Jesus was familiar with them all, and he said: "It is easier for a camel to pass through the eye of a needle, than for a rich man to enter the Kingdom of God." Even as in small towns today, so in Nazareth you could not accumulate wealth without the village folk knowing how you did it; nor could you spend it in riotous living without word being passed along as the women drew water at the well or the shopkeepers paused in their toil to pass the time of day with a customer…and Jesus observed and pondered on these things.

Although Jesus had the keen personal insight of a small town boy, he did not have the narrow outlook which we often associate with village folk. Jesus was well aware of the vast and complex Roman world of which Nazareth was but a part. As he looked out across the hills he viewed a vast panorama which was suggestive of the contemporary world, and when he journeyed to the Temple at Jerusalem he met other pilgrims from all over the empire with whom he talked. Quite naturally, therefore, when the time came for Jesus to proclaim the Gospel of the Kingdom he did not think in terms of Nazareth, but in such universal terms as "Whosoever cometh unto me I will in no wise cast out."…"Come unto me all ye that labor…" While the boy Jesus had undoubtedly gained the respect and admiration of all the villagers in Nazareth, they were not ready to listen to him speak "as one having authority." For them his humanity was too overwhelmingly evident, and made it impossible for him to be other than the son of Joseph, the carpenter.

At the time Jesus left Nazareth to be about his Father's business, John The Baptist was preaching throughout Judea the gospel of repentance unto the remission of sins, and winning a reputation as a hero because of the enemies he was not afraid to make. A man of unqualified convictions and remarkable courage, he demanded that people should repent so they would be worthy of the Kingdom which was imminent. It was to such a one that we are told Jesus went and was baptized. Why? It is hard to believe, as some would have us, that Jesus intended to become a disciple of John, for John forecast the coming of one greater than he, who would usher in the Kingdom; and I believe Jesus considered himself the chosen one of God from the very beginning of his ministry, which coincides with his baptism. Nor is it conceivable that Jesus went acknowledging personal sins as we normally conceive of them. However, at the Cross Jesus took upon himself the sins of the world and offered himself a ransom for many, so it is possible that even at this time in his own conscience he carried the burden of these sins and thus felt the need of baptism.

That the baptism represented a great spiritual experience for Jesus there can be no doubt, for it is recorded that he was immediately driven into the wilderness where he wrestled with problems. It was during this time that Jesus crystallized his conception of his Messiahship. His was not going to be simply a social gospel, gathering the poor people about him with promises of a chicken in every pot. Nor was it God's will that he should fulfill the ancient Judaistic hope of a conquering Messiah who would bring the nations of the world under Israel's control. The power he was to exercise was to be spiritual rather than physical, and his carrying out of his Father's will would not be dependent on his being kept from trials, suffering, or even pain.

When Jesus came out of the wilderness and down into Galilee, the first thing he did was to gather some disciples about him. In itself this incident may seem insignificant to us, but when we consider how these strong and fearless fishermen dropped what they were doing, left their homes and families without question and followed Jesus, about whom they apparently knew little if anything, we get an insight into the tremendous personality of this man of Nazareth. Nor can we possibly conceive of Simon, Andrew, James or John following without question a man of "frail and slender body," as Sholem Asch describes "The Nazarene." No, Jesus must have had a physically strong body as well as a spiritually strong personality.

From that time on Jesus and his followers wandered throughout Galilee, Samaria, and Judea preaching, teaching, and healing. The essence of Jesus' preaching was that the Kingdom of God was at hand. The one great need was that people should yield their hearts to God, for the Kingdom was to be the gift of God, and it would be religious and spiritual rather than political and economic. The Kingdom was not just a future hope, but it also had an element of immediacy. For Jesus taught that the Kingdom comes not by military force nor by angelic agency, but by the individual human being accepting and doing the will of God. When the individual does that he or she enters the Kingdom, for says Jesus, "The Kingdom of God is within you." Hence for Jesus the Kingdom comes invisibly like the seed growing secretly, like the leaven working in the meal. Humans will not bring about the final and universal triumph of the Kingdom, however, for this is to be the gift of God to humanity only as the latter cooperates and opens its heart to the divine purpose.

The teaching of Jesus was carried out mainly by calling people to share his life, and by his being what he was. His actual instruction through parables and other means was subordinate to this teaching by the life he lived. The teaching of Jesus helped people to rethink God, and lifted their eyes to guiding principles. His message was always down to earth and in terms of human experience. Furthermore, his teaching was positive not negative.. he took it out of the realm of obligation and placed it in the field of opportunity. This is best exemplified by the story of the Good Samaritan where the neighbor is seen as the one who recognized his opportunity to help rather than one who was obligated to do good.

Jesus' work of healing was as much an integral part of his ministry as was his teaching and preaching, and the emphasis which the Gospels make in relating these incidents is in the part played by faith…"Thy faith hath made thee whole…," "Because of thy faith…," "and Jesus seeing their faith…" There can be no doubt but that Jesus was extraordinary and capable of extraordinary things, nor can

The Uniqueness of Jesus

there be much doubt as to the authenticity of the accounts of Jesus' healings. For us they seem miraculous, but for such a one as Jesus, whose purpose was one with his heavenly Father, all things were possible through the power of faith, and the only unbelievable thing was that despite all his efforts to point the way, his disciples still lacked the power-giving faith. I have no doubt but what this same power is available today to anyone who possesses the faith. Most times, however, we go out of our way to apply natural causes and effects to what are in reality miracles. It is not possible to blindly wave aside the miracles recorded by the Evangelists as preposterous. That some of these arose from parables and were later turned into literal descriptions, and that others grew out of illusions or incidents that were only apparently miraculous is entirely possible, but it is equally possible that the man Jesus was able to perform many miracles which we cannot understand or explain through our present day knowledge, because of his faith in Almighty God with whom he had a unique relationship.

This brings us to the question of Jesus' conception of himself. Just how and in what terms did he consider that he had a unique relationship with God? Jesus probably did regard himself as The Messiah, but he reinterpreted the meaning given in the Old Testament. The term "Son of Man" appears so often in the New Testament that it seems improbable that Jesus did not use this in connection with himself. It was a term which is not capable of exact definition, and it is possible that Jesus used it to indicate to his closest followers his divine relationship as "Messiah" while keeping the crowds in general from jumping to the conclusion that he was the Messiah foretold by the prophets.

The term Son of God, which Jesus also used in regard to his person, did not necessarily involve assumption that he was of the same nature of God. More likely it meant that he was chosen of God as a selected child. Jesus spoke with absolute certainty as though he understood the Divine Mind at every point. No similar claim had ever been made.

When Jesus referred to God as "MY Father" he used it to define a distinct relationship with God which was both personal and unique although subordinate.

By the time Jesus went into the village of Cesarea Phillipi he was undoubtedly fully convinced of his relationship to God, and in fact probably had begun to see the necessity of Calvary. As he saw the end of his ministry approaching he was particularly anxious that the minds of his disciples be also clear on this matter; and so he asked the leading question, "Who do men say that I am?" and, "But who say ye that I am?" in all probability fully aware of the answer he would receive, but giving himself an opportunity to teach them that "The Son of Man must suffer many things."

The teaching of Jesus takes on an urgency and almost a sternness as they approach Jerusalem, for Jesus can feel his time drawing nigh and he wants to be sure he has at least planted the seed that will grow like the mustard tree. The Triumphal Entry into Jerusalem must have encouraged Jesus for surely among so many who sang Hosanna there would be some who would remain faithful even after his death, and carry on his ministry. Thus Jesus was able to ride to his impending death with a sense of triumph. He could not tell just what form the victory would take, but since he knew he was living and dying in complete accord with the Divine Purpose he knew too that in due time God would bring about the ultimate victory.

That Jesus could have avoided death is very evident, but instead he went into the Temple and drove out the money changers. This incident had a very real connection with his death, for he aroused the business interests and disturbed law and order.

Three days later Jesus and his disciples met together for their last supper. We cannot help but feel as we read the

The Uniqueness of Jesus

different accounts that Jesus at least was very conscious of the fact that this was to be his last supper with his disciples, and that by establishing this covenant with them which they would not understand until after his death, he would help them and all future followers to keep faith with him and to carry on his ministry. He was well aware of the fact that not only must he suffer, but the disciples would be persecuted too. It was a covenant of victory and promise but it would grow out of sorrow.

After the supper they went out into Gethsemane, and the agony that Jesus underwent there, as his disciples slept, is a familiar story…albeit a difficult one to understand. We have here an "eye witness account of the full humanity of Jesus," as Major puts it in his "Mission and Message of Jesus"; but more than that, for Major does not feel Jesus would have had the Gethsemane experience if he had been conscious of his Messiahship, whereas to me this is but further proof of the fact. Here we have Jesus fully conscious of his Divine Sonship realizing how important it is for him in all things to express the Divine Will. He knows that he will very shortly be arrested and put to death, but he must be sure in these last moments of freedom that this is his Father's will. It is not that he is afraid to die—no, it is the realization that it is "not my will, but thine, be done."

If the crucifixion which followed Jesus' arrest in Gethsemane had been the last page in the story of Jesus' life, his would be but the story of another historical figure. He may or may not have been remembered these two thousand years, but surely he would not have been the spring from which flowed the stream of Christianity down through the ages. A dead Jesus could have little effect on people and would be incapable of transforming their lives as he does even today. No, the grave could not contain the Son of God. While we may never know the mode or manner of the Resurrection, we must accept the transforming fact.

This I Believe

The story of the empty tomb does not stand at the center of the disciples' faith in the resurrection; rather the central issue was that the Spirit of Christ clothed in recognizable form, was present with them. Jesus projected himself in reality after his death, and the disciples recognized him as the true Messiah, revealing God to humanity and reconciling persons to God.

The reality of Jesus must be thought of as the totality of the influence of Jesus Christ on the world. It originated in the man Jesus of Nazareth, continued in the Resurrection and the Living Christ who influenced the early Church as well as people today. We should not separate the historic Jesus from the Living Christ, for the living personal Christ of today, the Christ of Faith, is a coherent continuation of the historic Jesus. Any portrait of the historic Jesus which does not inevitably lead us to the living Christ is inadequate. Any conception of the Living Christ which quotes Jesus as speaking to them in terms contrary to the historical Jesus is inadequate too. There is no Holy Spirit without Jesus Christ. The presence of Christ today is true only if it is continuous with the man Jesus, and produces "the fruits of the spirit" as it did when he walked among men.

It was only after the Resurrection and in the light of the Resurrection that our records of Jesus were put down. Without the Resurrection we probably would never have had the record. The Church as a living evangelical movement started at Pentecost with the presence of the Living Christ. Jesus' life, therefore, must be seen through the Resurrection; and the Resurrection must have been inevitable to his life.

As we come to know Jesus of Nazareth, and surrender ourselves freely to the infinite Love, we must take his purpose as our own…then he becomes to us no longer an imposing and attractive figure, but an indwelling and inspiring presence, the breath of our lives.

The Uniqueness of Jesus

God I hardly know, but Jesus I know, and one who knew him best declared that in Him the Word became flesh…and we beheld his glory.

This I Believe

Chapter 5

The Power Of The Holy Spirit

The Church was born when the Holy Spirit came to a group of twelve rather ordinary men sitting around a living room. The experience was so gripping that one of them went outside and made a speech to the passersby. What he said was so moving that three thousand of them are reported to have joined the church on the spot.

With that kind of power being released, the Holy Spirit is a force to be reckoned with. This is why it is so mystifying that the Holy Spirit should be so mysterious to so many Christians. It is the forgotten third person of the Trinity. When it is remembered it is often not understood. When it is understood it is often forgotten. Only when it is experienced will it never be forgotten again.

The Holy Spirit is the way Christ came back. It is the way he comes back. It is whatever it is that turns rather ordinary people like you and me into Christians.

The disciples who gathered in the room on that first Pentecost had no idea that God would come upon them in the way that he did. They had their preconceptions, their ways of relating to God that were very familiar and patterned, and undoubtedly they were shocked beyond words when the strange Spirit began to come in such an ominous way.

I am reminded of the story of a little boy named Angelo who lived in a small town near the Mexican Border. One day he crossed the border and came back with a wheelbarrow full of sand; and when the customs inspector asked what he was smuggling in the sand, Angelo quickly replied, "Nothing." So all the sand was poured out and sifted through before he was permitted to go on.

The next day the same thing happened, and so on through the third day and the fourth day, and virtually every other day besides. Each time the sand had to be poured out and Angelo interrogated before he could move on. "I know you think that someday we'll be careless, Angelo," said the inspector, "and that's when you'll smuggle something across. So as long as you bring sand across, we're gonna make you put it through a screen."

The process took place for five years. Each day Angelo appearing with his wheelbarrow and each day the customs people pouring it out, sifting through it, and then permitting him to go on, until one day when it came to an abrupt halt. Soon after Angelo began to show signs of prospering; and then he purchased a big home in the little community and opened a thriving business. One day, years later, the inspector who had retired met Angelo on the street, and so he asked him how in the world he had become so prosperous when he had spent so much of his time hauling sand across the border and never once was anything in it.

Angelo smiled and then said to the inspector, "My friend, during those five years, when you were paying so much attention to the sand, I smuggled 1,593 wheelbarrows into this country."

The little story is surely apocryphal, but in a humorous way it makes a point that lies at the heart of the Pentecost experience; namely, we grow so accustomed to thinking of God in a certain way, and to looking for God in a certain form that often we're completely caught off guard as to who God really is and where God can actually be found.

The God of Pentecost is the God of Christmas and the God of Easter—that is, the one who appears unexpectedly and who at first is not recognized for who he is. "Behold, I am doing a new thing," he said through the prophet Isaiah and again through John on Patmos, and in effect that's what he was saying and doing on that first Pentecost as well.

The Power Of The Holy Spirit

Let us go back for a moment and take a look at the scene when the Church was born. What the South Bronx is to New York, what the East End is to London; in fact what all inner city decay is to large cities around the world, the district called Ophel was to old Jerusalem. It was a section of narrow, slummy streets. The word 'ophel' means hump, and if you could have looked down upon this section of the city from the air it would have looked like the mottled hump of a camel. It was the haunt of hooligans, the domain of the dispossessed.

In all probability, most of Christ's followers, who were plain and poor people for the most part, lived or lodged in this disreputable district. On the top of the hump is thought to have been the house where lived a wealthy and influential man, maybe it was Nicodemus, whose spacious home was always a shelter for the disciples. In all likelihood in the upper room of this well furnished house, "in which they were all accustomed to gather," it all happened. Here, in an area of the city where the cloak-and-dagger atmosphere prevailed, he who had himself been born in a borrowed barn brought his Church to birth by keeping the promise he had made to his comrades on the night in which one of their number had "double-crossed" him.

Suddenly, some mighty power, resembling wind and fire, fell upon and filled those simple fellows, and they sallied forth among the crowds of Jewish pilgrims from all over the then known world, shocking some of them by the exuberance of their utterance, and surprising many more by their intelligent and understanding use of strange tongues. Out of the Upper Room, then, on the fiftieth day following Easter, called the Day of Pentecost, several men, who hitherto had acted and moved around like mice, for fear of the Jews, emerged like lions. Some devastating inner upheaval sent them forth, fearlessly and well furnished with truths and convictions, to revolutionize all life

This I Believe

and turn the whole world upside down. They were a company of simple fishermen; lawless political adventurers, living luckless lives in fear of what the Roman Law could do to them; carpenters, ex-publicans, women all changed as it were in the twinkling of an eye.

All of it happened in A.D. 33, soon after Jesus had ascended. It was the baptism of the Holy Spirit which he had said they would receive. John The Baptist had said that the Son of Man would so baptize them, and Jesus himself had, as John's Gospel records it, used the words: "I will pray the Father, and he shall send you another Comforter, that he may abide with you forever; even the Spirit of Truth...He dwelleth with you, and shall be in you." Here was the proof that his prayer to the Father had been answered, and that his parting promise to his followers had been fulfilled.

It is not in the least surprising that the men who emerged from the Upper Room became the objects of wide eyed wonder and wild surmise. The people of Jerusalem deemed what they saw and heard to be a sign of drunkenness, due to the potent sweet or new wine consumed in those days, until Peter pointed out that it was just nine o'clock in the morning. The tongues, the speaking while under great emotional excitement of some strange language, incidentally is a phenomenon not unknown to this day. It was common in the early Church. St. Paul knew all about it. Certain bodies of people today still manifest it.

Psychologists, of course, have attributed the strange behavior of the disciples on Pentecost to mental disturbance or hypnotic influence. But nobody has yet accounted for the fact that a lot of unlettered men, full of fear and cowardice and other human weaknesses, fickle and inefficient fellows, became healers of diseases of the mind and body, philanthropists and philosophers of faith, religious writers of the highest order, theologians, and preachers par excellence, even to the point of martyrdom. They, who had fled frightened from their Friend and Master on Good Friday, took their lives in their steady hands on Pentecost because the promised Paraclete, the Holy Dove, the Comforter, the Holy Spirit—call the heavenly visitant what you will—had come upon them and they had given him a home in their hearts and the mastery of their minds.

"You shall receive power," they had been told; and now the promised power was theirs to employ. They were drunk all right, drunk with divine power. They were, so to speak, "God-intoxicated" men. On the hearth of their hearts had been kindled the flame of sacred love. They were aflame with the Holy Spirit, on fire with devotion to God and enthusiasm for His purposes in the world. Pentecost was a baptism of fire; the undying flame of inspired enthusiasm.

The miracle of the early Church was a partial fulfillment of Christ's expressed purpose about setting the earth on fire. Of course, it did not involve all humankind, but there is no doubt that the fire burned brightly enough, in the lives of those who were involved in The Movement, to make a miraculous difference in the culture of the ancient world. What we know is that it was the incendiary character of the early Christian fellowship which was amazing to the contemporary Romans, and it was amazing precisely because there was nothing in their experience that was remotely similar to it. Religion they had in vast quantities, but it was nothing like this. Consequently, the Romans, even the best of them, had no inkling of what was coming in the message of the early Church. Ceremonies they had galore, even Julius Caesar being a chief priest, but religion in the first century B.C. had no stirring message of hope for the masses of Rome.

The metaphor of the fire would be meaningless without the fellowship, because it has no significance for merely individual religion, as it has none for merely ceremonial religion. The major power of Christianity never appears except in a shared experience. Much of the uniqueness of Christianity, in its original emergence, consisted of the fact that simple people could be amazingly powerful when they were members one of another. As everyone knows it is almost impossible to create a fire with one log, even if it is a sound one, while several poor logs may make an excellent fire if they stay together as they burn. The miracle of the early Church was that of poor sticks making a grand conflagration. A good fire glorifies even its poorest fuel.

A further consideration of Christ's metaphor helps us to understand the importance of each humble and unworthy member of the total flaming fellowship. Many, when they tell frankly how their lives have been changed, refer to the faith and witness of some wholly obscure person who had been the instrument of ignition. That is why the Church is so important and why there can never be a Churchless Christianity. There is no Gospel in general. What we have in fact is always the Gospel according to someone, somebody. William Temple in stressing the mutual dependence of Christian people once said, "It is by the faith of others that our faith in kindled."

Though Christ's statement of his incendiary purpose has been strangely neglected, there have been reflections of it at various high moments in the history of the Church. There is a hint of the central purpose in Romans 12:11 where it reads, "Be aglow with the Spirit." Dr. Phillips connects it more closely with Christ's purpose as he translates it, "Let us keep the fires of the Spirit burning." When Blaise Pascal needed language to express the vivid character of his life changing experience in November, 1654, he wrote in large letters, on his secret document, the word FIRE. In the succeeding century John Wesley picked up the same theme with the well known words, "My heart was strangely warmed." A prayer which came out of the anonymous depths of the Church and which has been effectively employed by Nels Ferre is:

"Come as the fire and burn,
Come as the wind and cleanse,
Come as a light and reveal.
Convict, convert, consecrate,
Until we are wholly thine."

Or again in the words of the Charles Wesley hymn:

"O Thou who camest from above
The pure celestial fire to impart,
Kindle a flame of sacred love
On the mean altar of my heart!
Jesus, confirm my heart's desire
To work and speak, and think for Thee;
Still let me guard the holy fire,
And still stir up Thy gift in me."

Only a faith of which such a prayer is a valid expression can make the required difference in any civilization. Mild religion cannot sustain itself because it cannot start even a tiny flame.

Much of our present danger is that we do not see our task in its proper magnitude. Even when we accept the basic figure of the fire, we tend to interpret our vocation as that of husbanding the little flame in the effort to keep it flickering a little longer. What we ought to know is that a flame cannot, by its very nature, be contained. Without growth extinguishment is inevitable, because with fire, there is not a third way. As salt cannot fulfill its vocation except as it loses itself in the meat, so fire cannot continue to burn unless it penetrates the surrounding combustible material.

This I Believe

The Church cannot fulfill its sacred vocation unless it is a penetrating force, as salt is, and the penetration cannot even begin unless the fellowship which is the Church has something of the character of an explosion. Little can be done with a smoldering fire; somehow there must be a blaze. But how is this to be achieved? We do not know all the answers to this practical question, but we know something. Since the starter of the fire is Christ Himself, our initial means of achieving a real blaze is that of confronting Him as steadily and as directly as is humanly possible. When the closeness of Christ is lost, the fire either goes out or it merely smolders, like the fires in the great swamps which are hidden from the sun. A Christianity which ceases to be Christ centered may have some other valuable features, but it is usually lacking in power.

To confront Christ is really to allow Him to confront us, both as a group and singly, for we are changed by direct acquaintance. If any sincere seeker will try the experiment of reading the Gospels for a year, slowly and consecutively, but above all, prayerfully, and also with an open mind, it is practically certain that something of importance will occur in his or her life. If you stay close enough, for a sufficiently long period, to the central fire, you are likely to be ignited. But since Christ is alive, we need not be limited to the written word. He is really as close to any humble searcher now as he was to Andrew and Simon by the Sea of Galilee. The history of the Church, in all of its most vital periods, has been a continual verification of the prediction that if anyone hears his voice and opens the door, he will come in.

Our difficulty lies in the fact that Pentecost, like Christmas and Easter, commemorates an event that not only occurred once in history, but that also brought something new and permanent into human life. The Holy Spirit, then, is here in the community of those who confess Christ to be Lord. It is on what someone has so strikingly called

The Power Of The Holy Spirit

"the hereness of the Holy Spirit" that we should concentrate our attention. Instead of praying and waiting for some sudden influx of power, we should—in the fine phrase made familiar by Brother Lawrence—be practicing the presence of God.

It would be an altogether ominous outlook for the Christian Church in this modern, God forsaking world, if it had for its resource only a traditional memory, and for its proclamation One who was here, but is here no longer; One who was nigh, but now is far off. Yet how different the truth! His Spirit is here—here for the resource of them that wait upon Him, here to confront men and women and to change them, if they will hear him and heed him; and here to supply every seeking and unsatisfied soul with "something better."

Providing POWER is God's business—receiving POWER is ours. "You shall receive Power" yes, but only when you have been prepared, and only when you are prepared, by practicing the presence of God, to put it to work for the greater glory of God and the good of all people.

Paul in his well known thirteenth chapter of First Corinthians writes in praise of love. He has been speaking of the gifts of the Spirit, and says all these gifts have their place when they are properly used. Then he goes on to say, "Yet I show you a more excellent way." Then through all the beautiful thirteenth chapter he explains that the greatest gift of the Spirit is LOVE. All the other gifts are secondary compared to the love of God shown to us in Christ Jesus. They are of passing worth, but the Spirit is most truly present within us when it creates in us that love which was Christ's. The other things will all pass away, but "faith, hope, love abide, these three; but the greatest of these is love."

The Power that can overcome the world is the Love of Christ and through the Holy Spirit that Power is available to us. Robert Louis Stevenson tells in one of his essays that when he was a boy, he sailed out for some miles to see the building of a lighthouse. Nothing would satisfy him but to put on a diving suit and go down to the depths of the foundation with the diver. When they stood on the floor of the sea, his companion signaled to him to spring onto a great rock which towered high above his head. Young Stevenson thought the man was joking, but the man repeated the signal. Stevenson made the jump and felt himself lifted up till he stood on the rock. He had forgotten that the water was a buoyant element—that a force in the ocean would support his tiny effort and bear him up.

There is a spiritual force—the Holy Spirit—that supports and enlarges our own feeble efforts. How often we forget about it, and let ourselves be frightened by all the things that stand in our way. It is time that we learned to trust this POWER, and it will not fail us. This is the truth that the first disciples learned at Pentecost, and it holds good now as it did then.

When I say "I believe in the Holy Spirit," I am declaring my faith in my own spiritual nature, in everything that Christ has taught me about God. I believe these things, not because of what others say, but because of what I know. Sometimes the Spirit comes in moments of high experience, sometimes in times of silent thought, but we cannot doubt its witness. When we believe in the Holy Spirit and follow its guidance, it will lead us in paths of righteousness and service to our Master.

Chapter 6

What Do We Believe About The Trinity?

The New Testament does not speak of the threefold nature of God. It assumes, as the old Testament does, that God is one, and that this is the basic truth of religion. Several passages in the New Testament, however, seem to look forward to the later doctrine of the Trinity. One is at the close of Matthew's Gospel: "Go ye…and teach all nations, baptizing them in the name of the Father, and of the Son, and of the Holy Spirit." (Matthew 28:19 K.J.) This verse bears all the signs of having been rewritten after Matthew's time—after the rite of baptism had been set in a fixed pattern. Paul tells us clearly that baptism in the early church was "in the name of Christ." That was the very purpose of baptism—to assure that the convert should acknowledge Christ as their Master and put their trust in Christ for salvation. Except for this one verse in Matthew the New Testament writers always connect baptism with the name of Christ alone.

Another New Testament passage that suggests the doctrine of the Trinity is the benediction most of us know so well. Paul uses a number of benedictions, but the one at the close of Second Corinthians has been widely adopted by the Church: "The grace of the Lord Jesus Christ and the love of God, and the communion of the Holy spirit be with you all." It is strange that while we all know these words so well and use them all the time, yet we cannot be sure what they mean. That phrase at the end, "the communion of the Holy spirit," can mean three different things: fellowship with the Spirit, imparting of the Spirit, union brought by the Spirit.

These meanings are all equally possible, and have all found people to support them. But if we think of other things that Paul said, we see that the last meaning is the most probable—union brought by the Spirit.

Paul speaks of the Spirit, as the bond of Christian unity. Even though they have different gifts, all believers receive the same Spirit. This is what makes us one. So in his benediction Paul is thinking not of a threefold nature of God, but of three things he desires for his followers—that they should have right relations with God, with Christ, and with one another. It is significant that Paul mentions Christ first; here we have the clue to the way his thought develops. "May you possess the grace of Christ," Paul is saying that if you possess the salvation Christ has brought you then the love of God will be with you, and you will be inwardly united through the Spirit. In other benedictions Paul speaks only of the grace of Christ; in this fuller prayer he draws out all the things he means in the shorter ones. Christ comes from God and works in us by the Spirit, but there is no suggestion of three divine Persons who are yet one.

The Spirit, however, is always connected in Paul's mind with God and Christ. If we go through all the epistles carefully, we find that wherever he mentions the Spirit, he speaks also of God and of Christ. "Ye are justified in the name of the Lord Jesus, and by the Spirit of our God." "Through Christ we both have access by one Spirit unto the Father." "There are diversities of ministrations, but the same Spirit, and the same Lord. And there are diversities of workings, but the same God, who worketh all things in all." Paul joins the three names together without any set purpose. Of its own accord one suggests another to him, just as when we speak of the stars, we think also of the sun and the moon.

The other New Testament writers follow the same pattern. Whenever John mentions the Comforter in his Gospel,

What Do We Believe About The Trinity?

he mentions also the Father and the Son. The First Epistle of Peter opens with a greeting "to the elect according to the foreknowledge of God the Father, in sanctification of the Spirit, unto obedience and sprinkling of the blood of Jesus Christ." (I Peter 1:2 K.J.)

We can easily see how the idea of the Trinity arose about 200 A.D. naturally from the study of the New Testament. Although the New Testament writers said nothing clearly and definitely about God's threefold nature, yet they seemed everywhere to take it for granted. They always related the action of the Father to the action of the Son and the Spirit.

We can also see how people came to think of the Spirit as a Person. In a very real sense all that is done by the mysterious power is personal. Christ comes to us through the Spirit. We have communion with God through the Spirit. We cannot possibly separate the action of the Spirit from that of Divine Persons. We have contact with them through the power that speaks for them. Therefore that Power must be personal too. If we stop to think of it, our human relationships follow the same pattern. We talk about the influence our parents have had on us. We don't think of it as something different from them, even though they may have died long ago and only their influence remains. That influence is nothing else than the abiding presence of our parents. At a time when we are tempted to go wrong, their influence comes in and keeps us in a straight path. It has this power over us because they themselves are in it. In the same way God is in his Spirit. Christ speaks to us when it speaks.

People did not need any theological art to discover that the Spirit was a Person and one of the three who could not be separated. We all feel this ourselves as soon as we think about what the Spirit does for us. Its voice is the voice of Christ; it supports our weakness with the power of God. Even in our thoughts we cannot separate it from living personality.

So while the doctrine of the Trinity has no place in the New Testament, it was bound to grow out of the New Testament teaching. Once it was adopted, it became the framework into which all Christian beliefs were fitted. That is, from the time of the Council of Nicene in 325 A.D.

The doctrine grew mainly from humankind's desire to declare, beyond all possibility of doubt, the divine nature of Christ. Christ had spoken for God because he was one with God. His action for the good of humanity had eternal value because God was acting through him. Religious leaders realized that if men and women were to have absolute trust in Christ, they must be convinced that in him they had access to God himself, and they were therefore to think of him as part of God's very being.

Some people have thought of the doctrine of the Trinity as mere theory. They say it deals with things we cannot possibly understand and that do not touch our actual Christian life. We must agree that both in ancient and modern times the doctrine has been discussed mostly in words and ideas that we cannot explain definitely. The ordinary person is inclined to feel that there is no need to waste time on such deep and difficult questions. Instead one should devote themselves to the plain Christian duties that can be understood. Certainly that is right. Intellectual riddles are worth very little unless they help us with our great problem of how to live as Christian men and women. But the belief in the Trinity is by its very nature a practical belief. The object of our Fathers in the Faith who formed it was to make sure we can depend fully on Christ. Then we will never doubt that his will is God's will, and all he did for us expressed God's love and purpose.

People have always found that when they leave the belief in the Trinity behind, something vital to them goes out of Christianity. Jesus becomes little more than a noble and respected Teacher, or one among many great leaders we

What Do We Believe About The Trinity?

look up to with reverence. They lose the feeling that his word is final and that we must surrender ourselves to him. Christian faith is the complete acceptance of Christ as Lord, and the doctrine of the Trinity safeguards this faith. So the doctrine that three Persons are united in the being of God, which at first sight seems so far from all the practical interests of persons, really gives strength to the faith they must have in their daily living.

In one respect the doctrine of the Trinity fails to satisfy us. It allows no real place to the Spirit, which remains a kind of shadow cast by the two actual Persons. There seems to be no definite reason why the Spirit should be there at all. Devout Christians are sometimes troubled by a feeling that they neglect the Spirit. They believe passionately in God and Christ, and they declare that this third Person is equal to the others in power and glory. Yet they find themselves praying without any thought of the Spirit.

We cannot help feeling there is something lacking in a doctrine that thus keeps the Spirit from being real to us. For the first believers the Spirit was the one thing they could be certain of. It was present with them. They could see it working and could feel it in their own hearts. The higher world was real to them because the Spirit, which came forth from it, was so real to them they could almost see it. It is strange indeed that the later doctrine should put the Spirit in second place, so that we do not feel sure it really exists.

The fault though, is not in the doctrine, but in ourselves. It lies in our failure to understand that the doctrine is something more than a doctrine. A statement may be true and we may fully agree with it, but it means little to us unless it answers our own needs in some way. Shakespeare observes that ideas by themselves cannot do much to help a person:

"O, who can hold a fire in his hand
by thinking on the frosty Caucasus?"

This I Believe

Just thinking of coolness does not bring it to you. Yet by this very method we sometimes try to be religious. Hold the right doctrines; agree to a number of true statements; and by this thinking about the truth we will come somehow to possess it. But this orthodoxy, this following of church creeds, is worth nothing at all by itself.

Our beliefs must enter into our life. We must make an actual contact with God before he can help us. We accept the doctrine of the Trinity, thinking it reveals God's nature to us and brings us into fellowship with him, while all it can do, taken only as a doctrine, is to help us in our thinking. We must grasp the truth which the doctrine contains and let that truth help us to know God at first hand for ourselves. Then we can see that the doctrine of the Trinity is much more than a doctrine. And only then can its truth help us in our daily living.

Those who framed the doctrine of the Trinity might have done well to begin with the Spirit instead of seeming to bring it in as a sort of afterthought, after they had said what was chiefly in their minds. "I believe in the Spirit" that is the very base, the very foundation, of religion. In the midst of this earthly scene I am aware of another world that I must live for. I believe in the Spirit because I know it as a fact. Again and again I have felt it touching me—in moments of exaltation or of quiet thought, in strange experiences, in the love that others have shown me and the love I bear for them. If a person has never known those impulses of the Spirit, everything else in religion is a sealed book to them. You cannot realize what it is all about, any more than a blind person can see the lake and the sunset when you tell them they lie before their unseeing eyes. It is the Spirit that gives us the power to understand all higher truths. Only when it touches us do we awaken to the presence of God and respond to the message of Christ. So we must not think that the belief in the Spirit takes second place in our faith. It is

What Do We Believe About The Trinity?

at the root of everything. "The natural man," says Paul, "receiveth not the things of the Spirit of God: for they are foolishness unto him: neither can he know them, because they are spiritually discerned." The first thing we must do in religion is to believe in the Spirit. When we have once done that, the Spirit will lead us unto all truth.

The doctrine of the Trinity, we see, owes all its meaning to that part of it which it seems almost to leave out of sight. We have a statement about the nature of God, but what is the statement based on? How can we know even that God exists? He may exist only in our imagination. He may be just another name for the universe that lies around us. Many people have held these views. Since God is hidden from sight and reason, there seems to be no way to answer them.

But there is one sufficient answer. Though we cannot find God out by searching, we know the Spirit. Its coming is a fact we cannot doubt. It speaks to us plainly of a divine power. Not only does it tell us that God exists, but it reveals something of his nature. Wherever people have believed in God, they have thought of him as holy and just and good—not only because they wish to think of him that way, but because they must. The Spirit compels them to think of God in that way and no other.

The Spirit also assures us of the relation of Christ to God. The idea that God was revealed in Christ might seem to be utterly without foundation. Many people have tried to show that this idea was nothing but a myth or superstition. They said it arose, like many others, in an ignorant age. But there is sure evidence for this idea. The early disciples believed it because they witnessed the works of the Spirit with their own eyes. We believe it still because we have fellowship with Christ through the Spirit. We find that his will is God's will. The more we grow like him, the more we enter into the divine life.

This I Believe

Even as the Spirit testifies to some inward relation between Christ and God, so it also testifies to itself. When it enters into us, we know that this is something out of a higher world. This power that guides us and sustains us and enlightens us is one with God and with Christ, who revealed him. In a real sense the doctrine of the Trinity is necessary to our Christian faith. It sums up the truths which pervaded all the New Testament teaching, though it may not be stated openly there. It is proved also by our own deepest experience of God and of the Spirit and of Christ. We know them as three and yet as one.

Tertullian around 200 A.D. thought of the Trinity as being somewhat like three different officials carrying out three different tasks in one and the same government. Athanasius a hundred years later likened it to the fact that the same man can be at the same time a father, a son, and a brother. And Augustine, a hundred years later still, compared it to memory, understanding and will, three different yet closely related functions within the same mind.

Still the doctrine of the Trinity helps us only when we look beyond its literal sense. It was drawn up in an age when men tried to state their beliefs in terms of reason, and this can never be done. We cannot explain faith or love by a mathematical formula, as we can a law of matter.

Those higher things, we say, are spiritual. We must feel them inwardly before we can understand them. This is supremely true when we try to express the nature of God. Many good Christians cannot accept the doctrine of the Trinity as it is set forth in the creed, yet they believe in it. They never doubt that God is over all, that he has revealed himself in Christ, that he comes to us in the power of his Spirit. They know that God and Christ and the Spirit cannot be separated and are one God.

The words of the doctrine do not greatly matter as long as we grasp their essential meaning. Indeed, one of the functions of the Spirit is just this—to take old forms and doctrines and help us to understand them so that they will have a vital meaning to us. We do not really believe until we can state the old truth in our own way and still find it true.

This I Believe

Chapter 7

What Is A Sacrament?

Why do we celebrate the Sacraments of Baptism and Holy Communion? What do we mean by them? What purpose do they fulfill? Why do we protestants only recognize two Sacraments? When we baptize a baby is it because we feel that without this sacred rite the infant is condemned to damnation? Or is it simply a service for the parents in which they are asked to promise to teach the child by precept and example certain things which for the most part they have never learned themselves? What goes on in the communion service? Is this some carry over from our primitive ancestors who ate human flesh and drank blood? Do we know what we mean by Transubstantiation? Do we believe in it? Or again, is the service of Holy Communion merely a symbolism for something we are not sure we believe in anyway? These are some of the questions I would have you ask yourself as we search for a growing understanding of the Sacraments.

St. Augustine defines the sacraments as "The Word made visible." The Word is Jesus Christ—the Word made flesh. In Scripture and sermon we "hear" that he gave up his life for us, but in the breaking of bread we "see" that his body was broken on our behalf. The sacraments exist to witness to him and his saving power. The Sacrament of the Lord's Supper or Holy Communion is not merely a "remembrance" of things past, it is a "recalling," a making present of the living Christ. A past event (the presence of the Lord with his earliest disciples) becomes a present event (the presence of the Lord with his contemporary disciples). The Word is made visible.

This I Believe

At the time of the Reformation the Sacraments were frequently described as SEALS. In those days when a king issued a decree it was not considered official unless "the king's seal" had been affixed to it. The seal made the proclamation authentic, and if it was affixed the hearers knew that the king himself was speaking to them through it.

In the same way, the Sacraments are seals. They authenticate the proclamation of the Gospel in Scripture and sermon. They make clear that the King himself is speaking to us, for they are his Seal upon what has been said. The promises from the pulpit are sealed to us by the action at the Table.

The Sacraments have also been described as "outward and visible signs of inward and spiritual grace." "The grace of our Lord Jesus Christ" is not just talked about in Protestant worship. It is given an outward manifestation. This is in keeping with Jesus' own ministry. He did not just talk about the Kingdom of God, he gave outward and visible signs of its presence. When he cured a leper by touching the leper and thus taking the leper's misfortune upon himself, he was giving an outward sign of what the Kingdom of God is like—that in the Kingdom of God the Lamb of God takes the sins of the world upon himself.

Christ has given similar signs to the Church. The Church does not just talk. It acts. It acts in the way its Lord acted. Since "the Lord Jesus took bread…" so does the Church. It acts in the way he told it to act. The Sacraments are the outward signs of "the grace of our Lord Jesus Christ."

Protestants are agreed in observing two Sacraments, the Sacrament of Baptism and the Sacrament of The Lord's Supper or Holy Communion. Unfortunately, this agreement is purchased at the price of disagreement with Roman Catholicism and Eastern Orthodoxy, both of which affirm a belief in seven Sacraments.

What Is A Sacrament?

The difference here stems from contradictory interpretations of the New Testament material. Protestants insist that Jesus Christ instituted but two Sacraments for his Church, and that these are explicitly set forth in his teachings. None of the other Sacraments practiced by Roman Catholicism and Orthodoxy (namely: penance, confirmation, matrimony, ordination, and extreme unction) appear to Protestants to have the same authority.

The Protestant Church does not believe that the Sacraments are optional appendages in the Christian life, to be neglected or received at will. This may come as a surprise to those who customarily stay home on Communion Sunday. Our lax attitude in regard to the Sacraments is due, in part at least, to the Protestant position that the Sacraments are not necessary for individual salvation. Salvation is a gift conferred by God and not by Sacraments. The Sacraments show forth or ratify or "seal" the promise of salvation, but they do not guarantee it. Only God can do that. But we make a mistake when because of this we permit a cavalier attitude toward them. The individual who neglects the Sacraments on the ground that they are not essential to their salvation, is neglecting the means God has ordained for the proclamation and reception of The Word, and in showing disdain for those means they are showing disdain for the God who provides them.

While we do not look upon infant baptism as a means of salvation from original sin, we would have to recognize that every baby is born in a world where sin is already rooted. From the very beginning of life the infant is subjected to the pressures and distortions of evil influence. A world full of hate and irritability, of pride and contempt, of cruelty and thoughtlessness, of sensuality and vulgarity, of cynicism and boredom, is a world of which every child is a member from the very beginning of his or her life. To grow up simply as a member of that community of sin is to grow up in estrangement from God.

In Jesus Christ, God has implanted another community here on earth. Jesus and his disciples are a beachhead of righteous love in a sinful world. If we are to grow into fellowship with God, we must be inducted into this city within a city, this redemptive community of the forgiven and forgiving, this fellowship of faith. Baptism is the rite by which the Christian fellowship acknowledges the induction of a new member into it. A baptized person still lives in the world, but through the Church as a community of faith God has claimed that person for his own. Although the baptized person lives in the world he has a better citizenship in the kingdom of God, and the Church has accepted responsibility for helping him or her to grow in this higher citizenship.

Later on, the child will have to affirm or reject this activity of grace. If he or she rejects it, this will not alter the fact that the deed has been done, and that God claims him or her and will always claim them. If they affirm it, and the reality of their faith later waivers, they will discover that the reality of their baptism never waivers.

The question whether total immersion, or the pouring of water over the head of the person to be baptized, or the laying of moistened hands on their head (sprinkling) is more effective in the enactment of the gospel, depends on the experience of the persons involved. Wesley wisely recognized this fact, and for this reason The United Methodist Church offers baptism in any of the three modes as requested by the person to be baptized or, in the case of infants, by his or her parents. However, sprinkling is customary and exceptions to it are becoming less common.

Baptism is the act of incorporation into the membership of the body of Christ, and as such it occurs but once. The Lord's Supper or Holy Communion, on the other hand, is

What Is A Sacrament?

the act whereby that membership is sustained and nurtured. As such it occurs many times.

It seems a strange thing over which to make a fuss, this act of eating bread and drinking grape juice. Surely God could have acted in more spectacular fashion. Whether he could have or not, however, is beside the point—this is how he chose to act. This is not God 'saying' what he is like, this is God 'doing' what he is like. Here the Christian Gospel is transformed from word to deed, from promise to actuality, from hope to fulfillment. God's forgiveness, to take one example, ceases to be an idea and becomes a reality. Once again we find that the reality is pure grace, unmerited, but given anyhow. Communicants pray: "We do not presume to come to this Thy Table, O merciful Lord, trusting in our own righteousness, but in thy manifold and great mercies. We are not worthy so much as to gather up the crumbs under Thy Table..." But on those terms we are welcome at Christ's Table, not because we have a right to be there, but because we can trust in God's manifold and great mercies. We are not refused because we are sinners. We are welcomed because we are forgiven sinners.

Through this Sacrament we are united with Christ. As we take the Bread and Wine into our physical bodies we indicate our desire that Christ, whom the physical elements now represent, may enter into us and dwell with us, so that we may be united with him and he with us. Rather than simply talking about it, we act out our desire that Christ "dwell in our hearts by faith."

John Wesley and Methodists generally have laid much emphasis on personal religious experience. It is natural, therefore, that Methodists have tended to stress that the Lord's Supper nurtures the communicants' experience of God's presence. The expectancy of such experience and frequent testimony to it by Methodists tends to give our thought of Holy Communion a realistic affirmation of God's

This I Believe

presence akin to the Catholic doctrine of the Real Presence. However, most Methodists would probably say that while God is present everywhere, we are more sensitively aware of this presence at the Lord's Table than usually elsewhere. We might even add that God gives a special blessing to those who join in this rite sanctified by Christ.

No other service of the Church brings such an experience of divine grace as Holy Communion.

Because of the very special nature of the Sacraments from the very beginning of the Christian Church persons were set aside whose responsibility it was to administer the Sacraments. This was done by an act of ordination where through the Laying on of Hands, a direct line has been maintained from Jesus through the disciples, down to the present. In The United Methodist Church the Sacraments may only be administered by ordained elders of the church except in certain situations which are carefully spelled out in The Book of Discipline.

Human personality will wear out unless it is constantly renewed. The need of renewal is as old as humanity, and is as truly spiritual as physical. Human beings must have bread and water; some have been known to go forty days without food, but not one-third of that time without water. Millions are engaged in producing, transporting, selling, and preparing the food that people eat each day. The renewal of the body is an economic and financial problem of the first magnitude.

The mind must also be fed. Countless persons are engaged in this enterprise. The process of education is a daily renewal of the mind, and every person knows how a mental task sharpens the wits and gives vigor to the mind.

No less keen is the hunger of the human spirit, and that Jesus had in mind when he spoke of himself as "the bread that cometh down from heaven." Christianity began in a great adventure of the spirit. In every age Jesus calls peo-

What Is A Sacrament?

ple to life, the most vibrant and abundant life, and he urges each person to begin where they are as the challenge of new life grips them.

In the early church people experienced the vital thrill of this new life in communion with God; that communion they knew in such rites as Baptism and the Lord's Supper. It was in such Sacraments as these that the spirit of the early Christians was constantly renewed. As they consecrated bread and wine and partook of them in remembrance of their risen Lord, he seemed to be present with them as he had promised he would.

In the years that have passed these sacraments have always been channels of divine grace, the means of renewal which the church offers to the spirits of men and women.

The essential relationship of the soul to God is here dramatically presented by means of a sacramental mystery. Thus the Sacraments are an essential part of full Christian worship, because in them the Perfect is not only adored, but approached and received under sensible signs. It is therefore a sovereign means to that created perfection to which God calls our spirits, but which by ourselves we can never achieve. It dethrones egotism, the inveterate enemy of the spirit of worship; and awakens awestruck gratitude and humble love by a method which even the simplest can appreciate, but which even the greatest saint will never fully understand.

If you would truly experience the presence of the Living God in your life, do no neglect the Sacraments!

This I Believe

Chapter 8

The Bible—The Word Of God

I read somewhere the story of a man who visited an Orthodox Church service in a communist country. He told how the Patriarch carried a Bible around for the people to touch. The Christians gathered there reached out eagerly to touch the Holy Bible as the Patriarch passed their way. Surrounded by a hostile philosophy of communism they loved their Bible, treasured it, revered it. However, they never opened the precious Book to read it.

Time and again we have been assured that the Bible is the Word of God, and that if we read it faithfully God will speak to us through it just as surely as if he had sent us a telegram.

The Bible is the place where men and women encounter the living Word. As we respond affirmatively to that encounter we become alive, we become new beings, we find our true selves.

Many have tried and failed in this endeavor. They have started out with every good intention, but have fallen by the wayside because of difficulties they had in reconciling some of what they encountered with their knowledge and understanding of the world; or because of boredom. I recall one of my early attempts at reading through the Bible when the geneologies and all the 'begets' and 'begats' proved too much for me. The trouble with me then, and with most people who give up on the Bible, was that I didn't understand how or why the Bible was written.

There are basically two different views as to how the Bible was written. One says the Bible was written by divine intervention. This view assumes that God used his writers as though they were merely instruments or robots emptied of their intelligence. According to this position the authors were writing the very words that God gave them, and therefore they produced works that were infallible. The logical corollary of this view is that the Bible is 'inerrant', that is, totally free from any kind of error or contradiction, equally authoritative in all of its parts.

This view of the Bible is the one I was taught as a child and was called 'fundamentalism'. Today this is the theological position of what we generally call 'evangelical protestantism'.

Today, along with a substantial majority in most of the major denominations, I reject 'fundamentalism' and take a different view of inspiration. A view which I believe to be Biblical. The record is clear, for example as to how Luke wrote. Luke specifically refutes the automatic writing theory by stating that he used various sources available to him. Luke 1:1-4 shows that Luke compiled his gospel. He tells us that his sources were human records. Luke wrote about 85 A.D., some fifty-five years after the death of Jesus. Memories were not always reliable. For example, Luke, Mark and Matthew all tell the story of the women at the tomb. Luke tells us they saw two men; Mark says a young man; and Matthew records it as an angel of the Lord. The details are not important, the important thing was that Christ was risen!

Looking at the Old Testament the Book of Chronicles clearly observes that it was a compilation from other history books. It was not composed by God or any one person. See I Chronicles 29:29 and II Chronicles 9:29.

If we keep our minds closed to the fact of compilation of sources our unbiblical attitudes will make us abuse Scriptures in ways that were never intended by the writers or the Councils who canonized Scriptures.

The first part of our Bible to have been put together as Scripture was the Pentateuch or the first five books of the

The Bible—The Word Of God

Old Testament. Scholars have identified at least three major sources used in these books. The "J" tradition, representing the southern records kept in Jerusalem. The "E" traditions were the records kept by the Priests in the Northern Kingdom; and the "P" or priestly code representing a later editing of the combined works of "J" and "E" about 430 B.C.

An illustration of how we are helped by knowing there are several different sources is the story of King David taking a census. II Samuel 24: 1-2 written by a source that approved the Davidic dynasty tells us that the Lord incited David to "number" Israel and Judah. I Chronicles 21:1 written on the other hand when the Davidic dynasty was frowned upon states the devil told David to take the census of Israel and Judah.

The Bible is a human text written by human hands from human sources about Israel's relationship with God, whom they experienced as their creator, judge, redeemer, and savior. Four persons face the sunlight as it filters through a stained glass window, and each one sees the sunlight, yet each may see the colors differently. Yes, our varied experiences and backgrounds color the light as we see it. So it is that Paul can say of Jesus: "This day I have seen the light of God reflected in the face of Jesus Christ." And at the other extreme Samuel's hacking the King Agaga to pieces before the Lord show the light of God having difficulty getting through.

All Scripture is not of equal value nor quality. We must learn to 'sift' the record. Martin Luther advised that we should distinguish clearly between the straw on which the baby Jesus slept and the baby. John Wesley was also discriminating when he stated that Psalm 109 is unworthy to be prayed by the lips of a Christian.

The authority of the Scriptures is not whether a passage is in the Bible, but whether it measures up to the Spirit of

Jesus Christ. Would Jesus have prayed the prayer we read in Psalm 109?

We do well to recall how the Bible was put together, how these various writings derived from various sources were finally collected into what we today call the Holy Bible. The first book accepted as Scripture was Deuteronomy. It was found in Solomon's Temple in 621 B.C. and claimed to be the word of God by a woman prophetess named Huldah. When Ezra read the Law in Jerusalem at the place called 'Watergate' about 400 B.C. he apparently read portions of the Pentateuch. This marks the date of the acceptance by Judaism of the first five books as the 'Inspired Word of God'.

The second group of Hebrew writings to be canonized was the Prophets. This consisted of four historical books Joshua, Judges, Samuel and Kings; the four Scrolls of the Latter Prophets—Isaiah, Jeremiah, Ezekiel; and the twelve Minor Prophets—Amos, Hosea, Micah and others. This group of writings was accepted as Scriptures about 200 B.C.

The third group was called the "Holy Writings" and included ten separate works—Psalms, Proverbs, Job, Songs of Solomon, Ruth, Lamentations, Ecclesiastes, Esther, Daniel, Ezra. Nehemia and Chronicles. These holy writings were added to the Torah by the Jewish Council in A.D. 90.

When the Christians comprised their canon they simply adopted the Jewish decision, and the books of the Torah became their sacred scripture too.

The New Testament Books were chosen over a long period of time. Though Paul's Letters were venerated they were not referred to as Scripture until about 150 A.D. The second step was the collection of the Four Gospels. These were accepted as Scripture toward the end of the second century A.D.

The third step was the long process of choosing the rest of the documents, and the canon was not finalized until the last half of the fourth century A.D. Churchmen debated for

The Bible—The Word Of God

over 300 years about the Book of Revelation. It was not until 327 A.D. that Athanasius of Alexandria listed the twenty-seven books of our present New Testament.

It is helpful to know that the choosing of the sacred books was not a matter of having certain unique books handed down from heaven on a golden platter. It was a difficult and arduous task. Furthermore, for some the canon is still not closed. Martin Luther said the letter of James was a work of 'straw', not worth being read. John Calvin said the Book of Revelation was unworthy of a Christian's time. I well remember a Professor in Seminary reminding us that in fact each of us determines our own canon for if we are honest with ourselves we would have to admit that there are portions of the Holy Scriptures that we neglect entirely thus in effect omitting them from the canon.

The purpose of the Bible is for us to experience the presence of God. We must be willing to be sensitive to the leading of the Holy Spirit. We must be willing to look at the historical events of the Old and New Testaments through the eyes of faith. I believe that the human authors of the Bible were indeed guided by the Holy Spirit, particularly in dealing with the spiritual insights, concepts, and revelational events which comprise its essential message. But I believe that God worked in the writing of the Bible in the same way that He always works: namely, through normal human beings who retained all of their limitations and fallibilities. So it is to be expected that the Bible will contain errors and contradictions, that it will reflect the primitive views of the universe which prevailed during the ages in which it was written, and that it will often be at odds with the more accurate knowledge we have today of the universe gained through modern science.

Also, it is to be expected that the Bible will show an evolutionary progress in man's ideas about God, from the harsh notion of a vengeful Deity in the early books of

This I Believe

Hebrew history, through the sublime ethical teachings of the later prophets, to the supreme revelation of God's love in the New Testament record of Jesus Christ.

Modern people with even a minimal education find themselves in a strange world when they read the ancient Scriptures. The people they encounter do not speak our language, nor use our intellectual viewpoint, nor explain occurrences in the same categories that we do. We all have some understanding of modern astronomy, and yet we find in the Bible accounts of the sun and the moon standing still, or the shadow retreating on Ahaz's dial. We all know something of modern biology, but in the Bible we are told that when Elisha had been dead so long that only his bones were left another dead body was thrown into the cave where he was buried, and when it touched his skeleton it sprang to life again. Later on we read that after Jesus' resurrection many of the saints who had long been dead, arose and appeared in Jerusalem. We know that our light comes from the sun, and yet in the Biblical story of creation we are told that light was created three days before the sun. Anyone knows that iron will not float on water, but the Bible recounts that an axe head floated when Elisha threw a stick into the water. We may say sometimes that we "feel like the devil," but we do not really believe that demons cause epilepsy, deafness, dumbness, blindness, or insanity as the Bible tells us. We scoff at the weird tales of space crafts and creatures from Mars landing on the earth and kidnapping people, nor do we believe the Biblical tale of a fiery chariot coming down from heaven to snatch a living man from the flat earth to his heavenly reward.

Yes, we honor the Bible, and know that in it are the wellsprings of the noblest elements in our civilization. We bow in worship before Jesus Christ, but we are honestly bothered by many things in the Bible that some would have us accept as literally true. We find it hard to accept the fact that

The Bible—The Word Of God

things we have learned to be true are not to be used as measuring rods for things we read in the Bible. We are asked to shift gears too suddenly when we turn from our ordinary intellectual pursuits to the ways of thinking that the Bible contains.

Our problem lies in the fact that we have not learned how to know our Bible. Most of us have started out by becoming familiar with some of the choicest selections in the Scripture. We learn several of the greatest Psalms, the Sermon on the Mount, the Ten Commandments, a few of the stories like that of Joseph and his brothers and the Good Samaritan. This is the Bible that most people know.

Sometimes we delve further, and puzzled by a particular book we discover what the book was really about. We learn what kind of a person wrote it, when it was written and why, and it takes on meaning for us.

The Bible is certainly a book of biographies, and often we find meaning in it as we acquaint ourselves with the various characters that are portrayed and the truths they illustrate. However, if the Bible is really to make sense to us we must be able to trace through the entire Bible the development of basic ideas.

We start with God conceived like a human being who walks in a garden in the cool of the day; one who comes down from the sky to confuse men's speech for fear they might build a tower high enough to reach his dwelling place. Then we follow the road that leads out from that beginning until in the New Testament God is revealed in Christ as the Spiritual Presence in whom we live and move and have our being. The name of this God is LOVE and his temples are human hearts. As we read our Bibles from this perspective, and in any book or passage are able to locate ourselves with reference to this progressive revelation that is to know the Bible and understand it.

This I Believe

When we understand that the demands of God in the Bible begin with tribal people and customs so that God equally hates David's sin with Bathsheba and David's taking of a census, and see in the prophets where righteousness was made central in God's character; and finally in the Gospels to see where the will of God is clearly stated as being that to please him men and women must be inwardly right in thought and outwardly merciful in the way they live, and to know the books and passages where these developments take place that is to know the Bible.

If we would know the Bible we must start with human suffering as a curse from God, with all trouble regarded as divine punishment, and then see wiser, truer ideas of God replacing more ancient thoughts as the Book of Job argues against the old theology, or Isaiah sounds a new note in the interpretation of suffering. We see suffering gradually redeemed from its old interpretation, and while some of it is still punishment, more of it is welcomed as spiritual discipline, and part of it is lifted into the glory of vicarious sacrifice. We see in Christ and the cross where suffering becomes voluntary sacrifice as the means by which God saves the world.

To be a Bible Christian must we think, as some suppose, that a fish swallowed a man, or that the sun and moon stood still at Joshua's command, or that God sent she-bears to eat up children who were rude to the prophet? Is that what it means to be a Bible Christian?

No, to be a Bible Christian is a much more significant matter. To believe in God the Father of the Lord Jesus Christ, creator, comforter and sustainer; to know moral demands and salvation from our sins through the power of the Spirit; and to live in undying gratitude which shows itself in service that is to be a Bible Christian. To have found in Christ, revealer of God and ideal of humans, one who calls forth our admiration, captivates our love, and crowns our

The Bible—The Word Of God

hopes so that we are led by him into a life which rises above anxiety and fear as it labors for the kingdom of heaven here and is assured of the kingdom of heaven hereafter—that is to be a Bible Christian.

To be a Bible Christian is to understand that the spirit and quality of Jesus' life were meant to be reproduced by his followers. The Master's life, like music, was meant to be reproduced. Just as a score of Beethoven, into which the composer's love of harmony was once poured, is meant to be caught up by each new generation and played over again, interpreted by organs, choirs, orchestras, old instruments and new ones that may be invented, so the life of Jesus was meant to be reproduced in all sorts of circumstances, by all sorts of temperaments, until the whole earth should be full of it.

Jesus thought first and foremost about people who were missing the abundant life. For him people were more important than anything else on earth, and if any custom, tradition or institution stood in the way of leading people into a more abundant life it had to look out.

For example, do you remember when the sabbath rule conflicted with the need of a man crying to be released from disease on the sabbath day. Jesus was determined that rule or no rule that man should have a fuller life, nothing else mattered to the Master, and so he healed him.

This approach to the understanding of Christianity could have revolutionary consequences in our social relationships. It means we are called upon to stand up and be counted. If we neglect or dim our Master's ethical and social demands Christianity loses its reason for existence.

Yes, I believe that it is impossible that a Book written two or three thousand years ago should be used in the twentieth or twenty-first centuries without having some of its forms of thought and speech translated into modern terms. Because a person says I believe in the immortality of the soul but not

This I Believe

in the resurrection of the flesh; I believe in the victory of God on earth, but not in the immediate second coming of Christ; I believe in the reality of sin and evil, but not in the visitation of demons; I believe in the nearness and friendship of the Holy Spirit but I do not think of that experience in terms of individual angels who would deny that such a person believes in the Bible. Those are precisely the things that the Bible is driving at and which I believe. Life eternal, the coming of the Kingdom, the conquest of sin and evil, the indwelling and sustaining presence and power of the Holy Spirit, these are the truths once set forth in ancient terms, but are still valid in our terms, and will also be valid in the terms in which our children and our children's children may express them. This is the Word of God!

Chapter 9

Prayer In The Christian Life

One day I said to my wife: "I want to talk with you about a meditation I am trying to prepare on 'Prayer'. What I want to say is very simple: 'Prayer is conversation between God and us. It is the meeting of God and individuals. It is a person-to-person experience. There are many words to describe prayer with God such as dialogue, rapport, collaboration, friendship, fellowship, communion.'"

My wife interrupted: "But these are abstractions."

I responded: "I know; I'm trying to get hold of the right word, concept or illustration that will illuminate what I want to say."

She quietly said: "Prayer is like talking on the telephone."

I began to think about that, and the more I did the more I realized how similar prayer is to talking on a telephone. Prayer is indispensable to the Christian way of life. You can live without prayer; many people do. But you can't be a Christian and live without it.

The goal for Christians is to discover the will of God for each of us in our particular situation. Prayer is one way to do this. There are other ways, of course—hymns, sermons, reading the Bible, friends, experiences. But prayer is our most personal contact with God. It is an experience in which the universal principles become particularized for us. General truths are set forth in the Bible and in many other resources. After we examine these we ask the question: "What does this mean for me? What does God want me to do?" In prayer we ask these questions and await God's answers.

In prayer we discover God's will for our lives. As someone once said 'Prayer is the Christian's vital breath'.

This I Believe

The purpose of prayer and the telephone are the same: conversation with another person. God is a person. I don't mean he is flesh and blood. But God is everything that a person is and much more. He can't be any less than human, because God created us. This means that he can feel, think, and make decisions. It means that God is in control of the universe he created. God can listen and hear what we are saying. He can think about it, make a decision, and give an answer. When we pray, we are in conversation with a person who can do everything we can and much more. We are talking with the Creator and Redeemer of the world. Every conversation is a two way process. We speak and we listen. If one person does all the talking and no listening, it is not a conversation, it is a monologue.

I am afraid that, for many of us, prayer is a monologue. We spend most of our time talking TO God. We need to listen to what he is saying to us. Then there is dialogue. He says to us, "Be still and know that I am God." What does he mean? Perhaps this: After you have talked things over with God, you may want to say: "God, these are the things I wanted to talk with you about. These are the things I wanted you to do. These are the decisions in which I want guidance. I'm going to stay here awhile in case you want to give me any answers right away. For the next few minutes I'm not going to try to influence you; I want you to influence me." Then sit quietly and think about God. Who is he? What has he done in history, in the lives of others, and in your life? Open your mind and heart to receive the presence of God.

The purpose of prayer and the telephone are the same: conversation with another person.

Experimental telephones have been equipped with televisions so that you can see the person with whom you are talking. Most of us are happy there is no television attached to our telephones. If there were, we would want a hand switch to turn it off at times. When we use the telephone we cannot see the person at the other end of the line, but we can know that person.

In prayer we cannot see God, yet we can know him. A few have experienced visions of God, such as Isaiah in the Temple when he saw the Lord high and lifted up. Or the lady who told me that in her sleep one night God appeared as a knight on a white horse. But these are rare instances. In them God comes in disguise.

Jesus said: "No one has ever seen God; the only Son, who is in the bosom of the Father, he has made him known." We cannot see God, but we can know him through Jesus Christ. We know that God is a forgiving Father. Jesus told the story of a man who totally disgraced his family. A defeated wreck he returned home to ask his father to hire him as a servant. His father received the young man with open arms, and rejoiced that his son who had been lost, was found. Jesus said: "That's the way God is. You can come to him with your shameful, shattered life and he will put it back together again."

On the other hand, Jesus has shown us that God is One who demands a great price. God asked the most noble man who lived to die a criminal's death to save a sinful world. Jesus said: "He who does not take his cross and follow me is not worthy of me." (Matthew 10:38)

The God with whom we pray is a seeking God. He came to us in Christ. His purpose is not to spank but to save us. His emphasis is not on punishment but on rehabilitation. He has come in Christ and we are to respond. We are seeking God in our weakness, and God is seeking us in his strength. For centuries people have cried to God for help. We Christians not only know the need for help, we also know that God wants to help us.

We pray to a God we cannot see; yet we know him through Christ.

Prayer is like talking on the telephone because we discuss all of life, and not just certain segments of it.

There are prayers of praise and thanksgiving. We look back over the past months and years and marvel at God's goodness. We get out the scrapbooks and look at the pictures. We remember the tough times when God kept us steady. We recall the day a loved one returned home from the war, or the day we learned they would never return, and the way God helped us through that day and every day since. We look at today and how we are being cared for. We read stories of the tortuous journeys people have made in escaping from tyrannical governments. We see how little they have and how much we have. We say with the Psalmist: "Bless the Lord O My Soul, and forget not all his benefits."

In the light of God's goodness and holiness, we are aware of our selfishness and sinfulness; and so we offer our prayers of confession. Our failure to live for God is one of the things we deal with in prayer. We admit our guilt, ask for God's forgiveness, and await his healing love. We say: "God, my sin has made me weak, please heal and strengthen me that I may continue to serve you."

We pray for others: our families, our friends, fellow Christians, non-Christians. Out of the knowledge of their needs we make requests to God.

We pray for ourselves. We talk over our finances. We ask for strength to endure the difficult. We seek the joy of His presence in our lives. Whatever our need, we are free to talk with God about it.

For many of us prayer is a strange experience. We are like a young child using the telephone. Normally the child may talk his or her head off, but the first few times they are confronted with the telephone they may become shy and awkward. By the time they become teenagers, however, the family often wishes they had never put the telephone in their hands. Practice makes a difference.

Prayer can never become a natural part of our lives until we place it in our daily schedules. John Wesley, the founder of the Methodist Church, once wrote: "Whether you like it or not, read and pray daily. It is for your life; there is no other way: else you will be a trifler all your days...Do justice to your own soul; give it time and means to grow. Do not starve yourself any longer."

There is another way in which prayer is similar to talking on the telephone: communication sometimes breaks down. You ring a number and no one answers. You try for several days before you get an answer. Or you may only faintly hear the other person. This is certainly true of prayer.

There are times when God seems to have disappeared. We know what the Psalmist meant when he cried: "Give ear to my prayer, O God; and hide not thyself." It is some comfort to me during these times to remember that the great men and women of prayer all admit to these times of void.

Communication can break down because of external circumstances. Perhaps we have not had enough time to stop and listen to God. Under pressure, we have spent all our prayer time in talking. Or our physical condition may be dulling our spiritual sensitivity.

Communication also breaks down because of internal circumstances. It is as though we had removed the transmitter or receiver from the telephone. In our selfishness we have cut off contact with God. Then we must reestablish contact through persistent prayer until our desire for God overpowers our desire for self.

Prayer was a power in the life of Christ. His disciples knew that he often got up before the sun and poured himself out in prayer before God. He prayed for his friends and for the ones who were to become his friends, and always something happened.

This I Believe

The disciples were convinced that a high voltage wire connected Jesus with the source of all Power. They wanted to know how to make connections with the Father of Light. They too wanted to be able to communicate with God. They wanted to learn how to get an answer to prayer.

One day, one of them said to Jesus: "Master, teach us to pray." In answer the Master gave them what has come to be known as The Lord's Prayer. These simple words, containing as they do parts from older Hebrew prayers, are a model. Yet Jesus did not intend for people to think he was giving them a magic formula for prayer success.

In the account by Matthew, Jesus first gave his disciples a warning before he teaches them. He says, "When you pray, do not repeat empty phrases, as the heathen do, for they imagine that their prayers will be heard if they use words enough. You must not be like them." Then on the occasion reported by Luke, the Master tells a story that may seem to conflict with this warning.

It is the story of a traveller who goes by night to avoid the heat and glare of the sun. The man reaches the house of a friend at midnight. The friend is surprised, but glad to welcome his companion of former days at any hour. After the first warm greeting, he hastens to fetch water and towel to bathe his friend's feet; and then as the traveler relaxes the host hastens to the cupboard to bring him some refreshment. But alas, the cupboard was bare. Quietly he slips out the back door and runs to his neighbor's home.

No voice answers his knock. He calls out: "Friend, lend me three loaves, for a friend of mine has just come to my house from a journey, and I have nothing for him to eat."

A growling voice comes back at him: "Don't bother me; the door is now fastened, and my children and I have gone to bed; I cannot get up and give you any." (Luke 11:5-7)

The man turns as if to go back to his home, but the thought of having nothing to put before his guest stops him in his tracks. Again he reddens his knuckles against the door. There is an outbreak of muttering inside. The door opens and bread is shoved outside to the waiting man, who ignores the remarks that come with it, and hurries back to his home. His shameless persistence has gotten him what he needed.

Plainly Jesus meant to teach that if a surly, half awake man could answer an urgent request, God is much more willing and able to answer those who beseech him. He was not painting a picture of God when he sketched the grumpy neighbor. He was simply illustrating his remark: "If you, bad as you are, know enough to give your children what is good, how much more surely will your Father in Heaven give the Holy Spirit to those who ask him for it." (Luke 11:13)

But the parable teaches more. It teaches that stick-to-itiveness is a condition of successful prayer. Here we find the apparent conflict between Matthew's account with its caution against vain repetition, and the Luke account with its direction to seek "shamelessly" until an answer comes. But the conflict is more apparent than actual.

The needy host kept repeating his plea, not out of a head filled with empty phrases, but out of a heart filled with urgent need. Words are buckets to carry meaning. There are times when they must be worked overtime to get the job done. The need faced by this man drove him to ask repeatedly for help. He was not like a man in an old fashioned firefighting line receiving empty pails from the left and passing them to the right. He was dipping each word into the well of his predicament. His plea meant something because he felt something.

An ever present danger in repeating a written prayer, even the Lord's Prayer, is that we will simply begin to pass empty buckets. The words only sound, they do not communicate. It was to this danger that Jesus addressed his warning. People are not to depend upon the form or manner of prayer, but upon God and his promises. The kind of faith that will not take "no" for an answer kept the man in the parable knocking. It was because of his shameless determination that the answer was given.

For two thousand years men and women have dropped their heads in shame before the Master's accusation: "You have not, because you ask not." Many of us know what we want well enough, but we are convinced that it will not do any good to pray about it. Or, if we do pray, we knock, then pick up the empty bread basket and head for home without waiting for an answer.

There is no need to be afraid to admit it if we doubt the power of prayer. The love of Christ accepts us with all our doubts and fears. Jesus knew that there would be times when the soul would rise up in the midnight of despair and go in search of relief. He also knew that God might seem to the oppressed and anxious soul like an indifferent neighbor comfortably closed up in the security of his own home, caring about none but his family within the walls.

In the parable, the householder got up and furnished the bread just to put an end to the disturbance at his door. Did Jesus mean to imply that God is selfish and only interested in protecting his own comfort? Not at all! But he does say that there are times when we are tempted to think of God in that way. The real purpose of the story is to argue from man's little to God's much. Note how Jesus ends the discussion: "How much more shall your Heavenly Father give the Holy Spirit to them that ask him."

It is not within our power to disturb God's peace and thus force him to answer our plea. In the parable we know what the outcome will be even before it is told. We expect it to end as it does because of our own experience. Perhaps we carry the memory of a parent finally giving in to a nagging request. In the parable we look for the logical outcome—the householder will get up to stop the noise if for no other reason.

Prayer In The Christian Life

But on whose experience can we accept the next declaration Jesus makes? "Ask and you will receive." How do we know that God is a Father who answers prayer freely out of a heart of pure love?

Jesus Christ says so, and makes no apology for his bold statement. It is on his authority that we accept these things intellectually. But it must be out of our own experience that we accept them emotionally and dynamically. The difference this can make has been highlighted in a story about a bishop in a liturgical church. For years he had gone at the appointed hour to offer the prescribed prayer. On one particular day he was weighed down under a sense of monotonous uselessness. He began to read a prayer in the silence of the sanctuary. He was alone. Suddenly an overpowering urge seized him, and he cried out to God in his own words: "My God!"

Then in a voice neither harsh nor soft, neither personal nor disinterested, answered: "Yes, what is it?"

The sexton found the bishop the next morning, dead, his face a mask of fear and astonishment.

The Creator of the Universe not only hears our prayers but answers them. The impact of this truth is tremendous when it enters our life through an experience of its reality. It will not likely scare us to death, but it will change our lives when we have a genuine experience of answered prayer.

Mark Twain said: "There are times when I have to take the pen and put my thoughts on paper to keep them from setting me afire inside." This is almost what Jesus is saying. Prayer will be heard and answered in those terms when the heart will no longer hold back the burning message of our need.

Flaming words from flaming hearts have marked the trail of successful prayer through the ages. When Abraham was interceding with God for the city of Sodom he was driven by his concern for the people to an urgency that was almost impudence. Hear him say: "Oh let not the Lord be angry, and I will speak yet this once more." Or Jacob as he wrestles in the darkness with an angel: "I will not let you go, except you bless me."

Or the prayer meeting of the early church when Peter was in prison: "But prayer was made without ceasing of the Church unto God for him."

For most of us our efforts at prayer compare with these like a painting of the sea compares with the ocean. Often we begin without conviction and quit without a struggle. We must agonize in an unceasing effort in order to get an answer to our prayers. Jesus does not explain. He might have reminded us that no intelligent person expects to get something for nothing; or that God does not do for people what they could, with effort, do for themselves. The truth is, he probably expects us to understand that the delays we experience are, in themselves, an answer to prayer.

Paul cried repeatedly for God to remove the "thorn." The prayer did not go unanswered, although the thorn remained. The very period which Paul thought of as a trying delay was being used by the Holy Spirit to furnish him with "sufficient grace" to bear his burden through to victory.

When we pray to our Father we must cut free of the modern attitude cultured by lotteries and giveaway programs. As George Buttrick once said: "God hates the blasphemy of the get-rich-quick." The gift is not offered to a selected few. Neither does it depend on the knowledge or skill of the contestant. When the need is real, a person may, through the work of Jesus Christ, go directly to God. He may need to give vent to a heart filled with thanksgiving. One may call from the darkness to get provision for a friend. He or she may call out of the night for strength and pardon. But whatever the cause, we know on the authority of Jesus Christ and on the experience of his followers that no sincere word addressed to God ever goes unanswered.

Prayer In The Christian Life

If a parent answers the requests of a child without cruelty or trickery, but in a way they think best for the child, what shall we say of God? Will he do less?

God has not rejected us because of our attitude toward prayer. He is still willing to give us even more than we ask for.

The time will come when prayer is no longer just a "P.S." tacked on the end of a long day, or a starter's signal at the dinner table. The time will come when we discover prayer as a line of power linking us with God, "For every one that asketh receiveth; and he that seeketh findeth; and to him that knocketh it shall be opened." (Luke 11:10)

Jesus understood what life is all about, and how to get the most out of it. That is why he taught his disciples to pray.

Here then we are at the heart of prayer. The God whom you meet is your Heavenly Father. Therefore, as his child, bring all your problems, all your desires, all your longings to him, asking him to decide what is your deepest need. In his infinite wisdom he will give you that which will be a blessing, not an evil to you. When you go to God in prayer, if you are truly sensitive to his spiritual presence, there will be times when all your problems and desires and longings will be forgotten in the realization that God is with you and nothing else really matters. Then, when your prayer is ended, you will be so undergirded with spiritual power that you will wonder why you were ever baffled by these problems.

Keep alive in your heart an awareness of the divine presence, not only when you are praying but throughout the day, and in the midst of this fevered generation you will move with quietness, serenity, and inner strength. The greatest men and women whom the world has known are those who have walked with God.

This I Believe

Chapter 10

The Church—Who Needs It?

In the dome of the world's largest church edifice, St. Peter's Church in Rome, is a huge circle of Latin words. The words are engraved in capital letters. Translated into English, this is what is written: "Thou art Peter and upon this rock I will build my church." We who stand in the Protestant Reformed tradition do not relate this saying of Christ to the papacy. But how do we understand it?

We gather in our churches for worship and repeat Christianity's oldest statement of faith—the Apostles' Creed. In unison we say: "I believe...in the holy catholic Church." Many persons would not say that; many church members would say: "I <u>belong</u> to the church," but find it strange to say: "I <u>believe</u> in the church."

Two questions are worth asking and answering. First, what do we mean by the term "church"? Second, who needs it?

What is meant by the word "church"? It may mean a building at a busy urban intersection, or on a village green, or at a country crossroads. It may mean a special polity or form of government and organization. It may mean the entire body of Christians—Orthodox, Protestant, Roman.

As Professor Donald G. Miller has written in 'The People of God': "The word "church" is a very flexible word. To some it means a kind of club or lodge. To others, an effective social agency, existing basically to serve the needs of the poor, the unfortunate. It is "the religious arm of the Community Chest...a Society for the Prevention of Cruelty to Human Beings." Still others think of the church as a religious clinic, a place where people come to get their problems solved. Others think of the church as a religious gymnasium where moral, spiritual, yes, and physical exercises

This I Believe

are available to increase the individual's moral, spiritual and physical health. Others think of it as a society to perpetuate the memory of Jesus of Nazareth as the Sons and Daughters of the American Revolution rekindle the memory of the American Revolution."

But none of these is adequate when you look at the church through the New Testament.

Look at the word for a moment. The English word "church" comes from a Greek word ("kryiakon") which means "That which belongs to the Lord." This particular word is used only twice in the New Testament (I Corinthians 11:20 and Revelation 1:10). But our English word "church" is used especially to translate another New Testament word which is closely tied to the idea of "that which belongs to the Lord." It is the word "ecclesia." This describes the "people who belong to the Lord."

Originally the basic meaning of "ecclesia" was a gathering of citizens, summoned, or "called out", by a herald to meet in a public place. It came to be used for any public assembly of people.

But the Bible gives a special meaning to the word. In the Greek translation of the Old Testament, you have the expression: "the ecclesia of God," or "the ecclesia of the Lord." There is a definite connection between the Church and the Old Testament people of God. Paul speaks of the Church as "the Israel of God." The new Israel, the Church, was created by the acts of God, by all that God had done in and through Jesus. Therefore, we may say that the meaning of the word "church" is "the fellowship of the Lord Jesus Christ."

In Emil Brunner's words, in "I Believe in the Living God," the Church consists of "the men and women who with him (Christ) form a living community as a body with its head, as a vine with its many different branches, the men and women who because they are united with Him, their heav-

The Church—Who Needs It?

enly Lord, also belong to one another and are dependent upon one another just as the members of a body and as the vital parts of a vine are."

This closely knit company of persons, joined through the person of Christ, may have buildings, organization, form of government, officers. (Of course, the Church can exist without buildings—as we have seen in China and Russia—but do not write off the external, physical environment. Musicians know that a symphony orchestra can produce a better performance in a good building than out-of-doors. Even so, in China and Russia once the restraints were lifted the Church began reclaiming its buildings.) But all that is not the Church; it is what the Church has.

The Church lives when God opens the eyes of a person to the true identity of Jesus of Nazareth. Peter was the first open believer in Jesus as the Christ, for, as far as we know, he was the first to make the confession of faith in Jesus as Christ, the Son of the living God. The Church exists where two or three or more recognize Jesus, the son of the carpenter of Nazareth, as Lord and Redeemer. Upon the rock of this confession, the Church is built. "Thou art Peter, the rock, and upon this rock I will build my Church."

What is the Church? The Church is the community of those who belong to Jesus Christ through trust, obedience and loyalty. The Church is the Body of Christ, the spiritual body through whom the mind of Christ, the spirit of Christ, the will and heart of Christ function. It is holy, not because it is flawless, but because it is not. We the members, are not flawless. It is holy because it is divine in origin and destiny, because it is "separated," that is called out to be God's people, Christ's servants. It is catholic because it is universal, world embracing. A cynic once said: "I believe in the church universal and regret that it does not exist." But it does exist, a potent reality, and is constantly realizing its unity and worldwide nature and mission. We use the word "ecumenical" as a kind of equivalent description of the holy, catholic Church. Everywhere in the inhabited earth the Church operates, and increasingly realizes her unity and her mission.

God wills the Church, and Christ loves the Church. But a power is needed to make this will and this love work among us, or there would be no Church. The Church is created by the power of the Holy Spirit. This was the meaning of Pentecost, which we now look upon as the "birthday of the Church." On that day the disciples became filled with the Holy Spirit and began to speak about Jesus with a new power of witness. Jesus was no longer merely a figure of the past. He now became a living power within each of them, and within the little Christian community. God in Christ now became a dynamic experience.

What happened at Pentecost was that through Christ Jesus the Spirit now worked in the Church in a special way. The Church became a place where the saving power of Christ became concentrated among persons. If we would find the power of God to change people and to change history, we must find it in the Church.

Pentecost was an astonishing event. When we think of those simple people giving a fearless and ardent witness to an inner experience of God, we are amazed. Pentecost marked the birth of a new community, a new order among people. What the disciples became was not due to their own merits. It was due to a Power outside of them that took hold of them and gave them new life. In a way, they began to become what Christ was and had come to share. What Jesus "began to do and teach" was now continued in a new way. Jesus promised to send his disciples a "substitute" in his place—the Holy Spirit. At Pentecost this promise was fulfilled. Jesus became present in a new way.

Through the power of the Spirit, Christ came alive in the hearts and minds and wills of his people. Christians now

The Church—Who Needs It?

received the gifts of the Holy Spirit—the very qualities of Christ himself. Through the Spirit they were given the power to pray, to love one another, to understand the things of Christ, and to witness for him. They became a meaningful, missionary, and hopeful company. The Spirit helped them to make right choices. The Spirit created the Church: the Spirit gave the Church understanding and power. Love, joy, peace, patience, kindness, goodness, faithfulness, meekness, and temperance—these are the fruits of the Spirit.

Today we greatly need to renew the life of our churches. Many people believe in God and in Jesus, but they have not had an inner experience of the Holy Spirit. They lack the enthusiasm, the inspiration, and the power the apostles had. When a church is no longer filled with the power of the Holy Spirit, it is no longer Christ's Church. It may have the outward form, but it lacks the inner quality of Pentecost.

So much for the question: "What is the Church?" The second question sounds flippant, even frivolous. Part of our present day humor shines through in the question: "Who needs it?"

Many persons outside institutional religion ask the question seriously. "The church, who needs it?" Some of these persons are aware that many of the functions and services once rendered by the Church, and some still offered, may be done more efficiently and with less personal involvement by community or government agencies. They point to another fact. Many communities seem overly organized. There is a club, a society, a league, an association, a fraternity or sorority for about every imaginable interest. We may join clubs to help us buy books or videos or invest our money.

A cartoon showed a young lady speaking to a friend on the telephone: "We're going to have a New Year's Eve party for people who hate New Year's Eve parties."

So, to some persons, the Church is just another thing to do, another organization to join. P.T.A., League of Women

This I Believe

Voters. Little League, Civic Music Association, Community Chest, Red Cross, Women's Clubs, bridge club, reading club, political party, business or professional association, Rotary, Kiwanis, Lions, church. Who needs the Church? Those who have a need for it, perhaps; who are not too greatly involved in other good organizations.

Who needs the Church? Every man, every woman, every boy, every girl needs the church! Why? Because the Church is the gift of God to His human children.

The Church is not just another organization of idealistic people, of sincere or insincere "do-gooders." It was not created by a group of religious people who banded together to form it.

Through the resurrection of Jesus Christ, God created the Church. Therefore, the men and women outside the Christian Fellowship need it in order to have the new life, eternal life, open to all who receive it by their trusting faith.

Professor Gordon Allport of Harvard University reported that a survey showed that two-thirds of war veterans indicated a "need for religion in their lives." Can't they find religion and be religious outside the visible church? A small girl's comment is relevant. One lovely Sunday, a family of four—father, mother, older boy, little girl—walked by a church on their way to the shore, the amusement park, and the beach. The little girl was attracted by the church, and was very curious about what went on inside it. A rather long discussion ended with the father saying: "Oh, come on: we can sing hymns and pray and worship God just as well on the beach as we can in church." "But, daddy," protested the youngster, "we won't, will we?"

No matter what splendid things a person can do alone, the fact is they don't usually do them alone.

Why do men and women and boys and girls need the Church? Because God has made us for himself, and we find Him, or, rather are found by Him, when we consciously respond to His call and come with others to praise Him, to pray to Him, to listen to His Spirit speaking to us through scripture and sermon and the other acts of Christian worship. We live fragmented, divided, sometimes torn lives. We need the wholeness which the Gospel offers.

Yes, we must confess sadly that, as a Church, we do not always let the Good News get through clearly. There are silences in our transmission of the Word of God. Sadly too, we confess that our local expression of the great Church is marred and often hurt by pettiness, unbaptized egotism, snobbishness, cynicism, and "short cuts to cheap grace."

Said John Burroughs, the naturalist, of a sanctuary: "I come here to find myself; it is so easy to get lost in the world." We come into the sanctuary that we who are so easily lost may be found; that we who so often sin may be forgiven; that we who are so often bruised may be healed. Who needs the Church? The community, local and national and world-wide, needs the Church.

J. Irwin Miller, the first layperson ever elected president of the National Council of Churches, once said: "No one of us, observing much human conduct, will deny that some word of effective warning and reproof is needed, and who is to give that word if the Church does not? No one of us observing businessmen conspiring to violate the law, labor leaders enriched and unchecked in their corruption, universities urging high spiritual values and illegally recruiting athletes...can deny that someone needs to speak out, and who if not the Church?"

The ruin of the Church means the ruin of the nation. It is not civilization and culture, not natural resources and technological brilliance, but only love, disinterested, sacrificing, selfless, that can unite us and make and keep us strong. This love Jesus gives us, and we experience it, are nourished by it, in his community—the Church.

Who needs the Church? Every community that would maintain itself in justice, in brotherliness, in true health.

I once served on a committee of Rotary International to select one of several young people nominated for a high award. What impressed me, as I studied the recommendations, was the fact that , without exception, community service and community leadership were matched by active participation in a church or synagogue.

From the doors of the Church go men and women, who with all their human faults, have had their vision clarified by encounter with God, their sense of responsible Christian citizenship deepened, their ideas fertilized. Said William Penn: "Men will ultimately be ruled either by tyrants or by God."

Who needs the Church? The Christian needs the Church!

A Christian is always a member of the community of Christ or he or she is no Christian.

No one can really be an individual Christian. When you cut off an individual arm or hand, the arm or hand is dead. We may need to change the structure of the organization through which the Church functions; but we cannot dispense with the Church. Every Christian needs what he or she can only find with other Christians. We need the worship of the Church; we need the assurance of Christ that our lives do not consist in the abundance of things we temporarily possess. We need the comfort of the Church's ministry. Comfort means "shared strength."

The famous Scottish scholar, John Baillie, said: "I cannot be a Christian all by myself. I cannot retire into my own shell or to my own corner. I cannot live a Christian life there." A single individual cannot be a Christian in his or her own singleness. A solitary Christian is a contradiction in terms. "Now you are the body of Christ and individually members of it." (I Corinthians 12:27)

Being a Christian is a lonely matter. No one else can become religious for us. Nor can we have what Christianity has to offer unless we commit ourselves personally to God. It is the Church's major task to insist on personal Christianity. But Christianity is not a purely personal matter. No one becomes a Christian by themselves. They receive the Gospel from Christians of past centuries. The Church has preserved Christianity. It brought the books of the Bible together under the inspiration of the Holy Spirit. Though an individual may read the Bible alone, they must remember its books would not have been canonized, preserved, or translated except for the fellowship of the Church. And unless one goes to Church they may interpret the Bible rather badly.

The Christian individual needs the correcting and challenging discipline of the Christian group. Church fellowship still has the power to keep the Christian from doing wrong.

It also has a prodding effect upon people who are spiritually dull. Its high demands on the Christian's life produce much self-sacrifice. In the battle against evil the Church is an "armory" for those who are putting up a loyal fight for righteousness.

Where two or three Christians are gathered, there in the midst is the presence of Another. When they gather together in a fellowship of truth, love, faith and hope they experience a group spirit that kindles the loyalty and devotion of each of them. The Church is the center of holy memories, the house of continuous prayer, the treasury of great tradition, the community where we find it easy to catch the meaning and the power of the Christian faith. Through the spirit, worship, prayer, music, fellowship and creeds of the Church each of us knows Christianity from the inside.

The distinctive thing about the Church is that it is God's creation. It is His beloved community on earth. It is His means of calling men and women into fellowship with Himself and with each other in grace and truth. The center of the Church is Jesus Christ. In the Church, God in

Christ dwells with His people in the Spirit, and through it, people find comradeship in a common witness and service to the Gospel.

When we will confess that Jesus is the Christ, the Son of the Living God, then it is possible for us to become part of the chosen community of God, the Church of Jesus Christ, which is so firmly established on the rock of the Apostles' Faith that even the gates of hell cannot prevail against it. The Church may be attacked, restricted, mocked, hated, oppressed. Its organization may be ruined, its buildings destroyed. Yet the Church of Jesus shall remain. Why? Because it is the only community founded on God's love, the love God alone can give and which he does give through Jesus Christ and his Holy Spirit.

Chapter 11

The Importance of Sunday School

In the year 1780, a man in England named Robert Raikes, editor of the Gloucester Journal, started a movement which was to have a far reaching effect on the moral and religious life of the western world. He began the Sunday School. He employed four women and on Sundays they gathered a group of children together to instruct them in reading and the church catechism.

To us that would seem like a worthy endeavor, especially when you realize that few of the lower social classes knew how to read and write and were scorned by the established church as something less than teachable. Nonetheless this Sunday School met with opposition from two sources. On the one hand, the ruling classes opposed the idea because they felt that it would lead to popular education which in turn would lead to revolution. And indeed it did in terms of the Wesleyan revival which came during those years. The other opposition was from the religious wing known as Sabbatarians, who enforced strict sabbath observance along Old Testament lines. Sunday was for worship and rest only and not recreation or work or school.

The process of Christian education which the Sunday School fosters began 2000 years ago with a man named Jesus who was called rabbi or teacher. He taught his disciples and anyone else who would listen. The disciples in turn became teachers and developed 'discipleship' as a learning process. The historical record reports: "Then day after day in the temple and in people's houses, the apostles continued to teach unceasingly and to proclaim the good news of

Jesus Christ." That process has continued unabated since that time. Christian faith requires a lifetime of learning for each of us, and the Sunday School is a primary means for this process of teaching/learning in Christ's name.

Even though most persons would agree that there is merit in the Sunday School as an educational factor in our culture, we have to face up to the fact that the Sunday School has fallen on hard times in terms of response. A general decline in enrollment and attendance has plagued all the mainline denominations. We can measure the results with tragic ease.

We have produced a generation or two of religious illiterates. One cannot assume a knowledge of the Bible on the part of the average young adult, or youth or child today. Biblical allusions and language are to be found in all literature, but many do not know that they are biblical in origin. There is much ironic humor about this. Take the old story of the preacher who was visiting a junior Sunday School Class and asked a boy: "Who made the walls of Jericho fall down?" The boy answered stoutly: "It wasn't me! I didn't do it." The preacher looked at the teacher who quickly said: "He's a good kid. If he said he didn't do it, he didn't." Then the preacher told the department superintendent about it. He said: "I know both the boy and his teacher. I am sure that neither of them would go around knocking down walls." In desperation the preacher went to the chairman of the church board, who when he heard about it said: "Forget it. We'll vote the money to repair the damage and take it out of our maintenance fund." You see what I mean about illiteracy?

The decline of the Sunday School has led to a failure on the part of many people to find faith in God as a sustaining power in life. Many of us came into our relationship with Christ and the church through our participation in Sunday School. Without it, many of us would not be professing

The Importance of Sunday School

Christians, and thus would be robbed of the spiritual dynamic which Christian faith brings into our lives.

One sees the negative results of this decline in our society which witnesses day by day a drift away from character growth and Christian moral standards. The low level of cultural morality in our nation has come during the period of the decline in Sunday School, and this is no coincidence. Our culture has moved precariously near the brink of complete moral collapse. Could it be that we have failed to be exposed to those lessons in living which Jesus came to teach us? I think there is a direct correlation between the two.

It is no revelation that we live in an increasing secularized culture in which, so much of life is lived without any reference to God. We have rightly claimed the separation of Church and State, but what has happened is that the moral element of State has also been removed in thinking and practice. Outside the Church and the Christian home, there is little effort to provide Christian nurture and moral training. If it isn't done here, it won't be done.

One does not have to argue the need for spiritual nurture among our young any more than it has to argue the need for education. We are raising what General Bradley called a generation of nuclear giants and ethical infants. No civilization can last long without the character that comes from spiritual nurture. We need to realize before it is too late, if it isn't already, that the Sunday School is the last bastion of moral sanity, the last best hope for spiritual values in our culture, and the finest opportunity we have for teaching about the way of Jesus.

This is a lifetime process. One does not graduate from the Sunday School, although many have tried to do so. Increasingly one hears adults talking about the importance of the Sunday School for our children and youth. To be sure! Yet the training of Christian character is a process that must go on through all the years of adulthood. One does not "learn Christ" in his or her first sixteen years and then assume that they have enough moral and spiritual knowledge and faith stored up in a personal computer to last a lifetime. If we could convince young adults and older adults that they are still teachable and that they must continue to be learners in the school of Christian living, we would move a long way toward emerging from the moral morass and spiritual desert in which we find ourselves as a society today.

The fact that you one day committed your life to Christ is not the end of the experience. That was the day of your beginning in Christ's school, and you will never learn it all, regardless of how many years you attend. The Christian faith is not an instant faith as some people would have us believe. One does not turn on to Jesus and immediately find oneself literate in biblical understanding or a finished product of spiritual vitality. All of us must think and study and read and listen and discuss the Christian faith if we are to know and experience something more than a shallow, surface religion.

The Sunday School is a unique institution in our society. It has had a role to fill which no other institution does or even can fill. It provides Christian education. The education provided in public schools by law must be a secular form of education, but many of our schools have gone farther than they need to go to avoid merging the things of State and the things of Church. Religion as a part of our culture is not outlawed in its teaching. Religious literature as a part of the study of the arts and sciences is not in violation of the Constitution. Moral values should be taught in cultural terms at least or else we sell out to a godless form of teaching which becomes a religion in itself. I even understand that in some places they distort history by omitting the religious motivation which led the pilgrims and others to found our great nation.

The Importance of Sunday School

The Sunday School supplements the secular education of the public schools, and if there is any truth in the assertion that some change history to avoid all religious references then there will be instances when the Sunday School must correct secular education. And we are cheating our children and ourselves whenever we fail to use the unique resources the Sunday School offers us. No parent would willingly cheat his or her child of the health resources our society provides. No thinking parent would keep their child away from school and thus rob him or her of the education which society provides. Yet how many millions of parents give no thought to the fact that they are robbing their children when they withhold from them the opportunity to learn the basis of moral character and spiritual values. It takes more than secular education to assure the survival of civilization.

The Sunday School, moreover, provides the means for developing Christian character. Education without morality dooms any society. Listen to Justice Jackson's warning, issued during the Nuremberg trials of the Nazi war criminals: "it is one of the paradoxes of our time that modern society needs to fear only educated persons. Only well educated and technically competent persons can destroy civilization. Knowledge can make the cad obnoxious and the crook more deceptive. If he speaks seven languages, the liar can lie in seven languages. Knowing the tricks of the stock exchange, the gambler who operates there can become a total parasite on society. Education is not enough. Educated men staffed the atomic plants and designed the Buchenwald furnaces. Educated students steal examination questions and stagger home from dances."

What do we mean by Christian character training? Dr. John Peating wrote: "The Christian character is one that is organized consciously around the will of the Christian God. In fellowship with the Father, the Christian finds the renewal, the reinforcement, the forgiveness, the leadership, the permanence, and the ideal companionship that is essential for the achievement of the social ideals of Jesus Christ." That is the goal of our Sunday School programs of Christian nurture. To develop that kind of Christian character, or to make possible its growth and development in children, youth, and in adults is what Sunday Schools are trying to do.

Sunday School teaches the biblical truths which provide the Christian resources for vital living. The Bible is our textbook for knowing the way of Christ. Sunday Schools use other materials which supplement these teachings, but it is the Bible around which all the teaching clusters. It helps us to understand God. It helps us to know his way. It reveals to us the depth and dimensions of his love. And it clearly sets forth God's divine demands upon us as his children. You could, of course, learn this elsewhere, but where else is this the primary text than in Sunday School? It is our resource book for Christian living. Sunday School helps us learn what the Bible has to say to us in our time and in our situation.

Another function of the Sunday School is to encourage spiritual growth. Again I would stress that we are talking about a lifetime process. It takes a long time to develop Christian discipleship. Growth in Christian faith and character may be compared to the growth of an atoll in the South Pacific. The island below the surface of the ocean rises slowly as coral, layer by layer, gathers on it. Finally, the island breaks through the surface and can be seen by the naked eye. This happens only because of the slow but steady deposits that have been swept across the ocean and settled upon it. Such could be the impact of Christian nurture on your life and mine. The coral of Bible study, layer by layer, year by year, gathers Christian truth in our minds and hearts, and the island of our faith slowly rises to the surface of our lives to emerge as the place of our faith and practice.

The Importance of Sunday School

More and more churches are adding adult classes to their Sunday Schools. Still it would appear that the great majority of adult church members ignore these opportunities. Perhaps it is because they do not feel the need to add to their fund of spiritual knowledge; or maybe they think learning is kid stuff. Dr. Harry Overstreet, a social scientist and psychologist, wrote: "An adult who ceases after youth to unlearn and relearn his facts and to reconsider his opinions is like a blindfold person walking into a familiar room where someone has moved the furniture. Furthermore, he is a menace to a democratic society." These are strong words. But what of the person who is a religious neurotic? His or her spiritual development was arrested at the infantile level, and he or she has failed to grow in spiritual knowledge or experience since that tragic moment. Not all non-Sunday School attendees are in this group, thank goodness; but the group includes many of them, and our question is simply: "Have I stopped exposing my mind to religious learning and spiritual nurture in the Christian faith?" "No," say the adult apostles who continued teaching and learning as they led other adults into the School of Christian living.

We are called of God to expose our minds and our spirits to the mind and spirit of Jesus Christ who revealed what God is and does and wants us to do. This calls for each of us to engage in systematic study of biblical truth and biblical applications of God's truth to the human situation. It requires of us an honest search for how that truth may be applied to our lives. The church responds by providing a process whereby that search is graded to growing persons. One method for children, another for youth, yet another for adults. And we all need this.

Another important thing the Sunday School does is to cooperate with families in Christian nurture. The family is the bane and the blessing of the Sunday School. By that I mean it is the bane, the frustrating bane, when parents fail to participate in the process. There are persons who want their children to be exposed to the Sunday School, but they disavow any responsible part for themselves as parents. There are parents who are willing for their children to be involved in Sunday School if somebody else takes care of getting them there. Others see it as a chance to get a little peace around the house by sending the kids off to church, little realizing that by staying home from church themselves they are negating much of what the Sunday School is trying to teach. An important ingredient of Sunday School is the participation of a parent or a set of parents and the home.

On the other hand, the family is the blessing of the Sunday School when the parents and the children realize we are all in this process together. Such parents don't send their children; they bring them. They don't assume that the church will take care of all the teaching; they accept their share of the task of nurture in the name and spirit of Christ. What a joy to teachers and leaders in the Sunday School when parents are vitally interested in their children's religious training. The secret of Christian nurture is not merely in the Sunday School, but in the combination of church and home sharing the task together.

Yes, I believe in the importance of the Sunday School as an extremely important tool to help us develop Christian character, to teach the way of Christ, to bring our minds into regular contact with God's truth, to cultivate the growth of the spirit, and to provide the biblical resources for faith and life to children and to youth and to adults. Through the Sunday School we perpetuate the tradition and practice which was begun so long ago when the apostles continued "to teach unceasingly and to proclaim the good news of Jesus Christ."

Chapter 12

Spiritual Healing

Time Magazine once reported that a committee of the United Lutheran Church in America warned the church's two and a half million members to steer clear of "Faith Healers," and accused them of Religious Quackery. Despite this warning, services of Spiritual Healing are presently being held in almost every denomination.

For some time now we have been witnessing a revival of interest in spiritual healing. We read of faith healing in newspapers. We read about it in magazines, and we listen to its strident appeal on radio and television.

In some parts of the country canvass tents holding ten to twenty thousand persons are crowded nightly by an emotion swept mass of people. Little attempt is made to exemplify the pattern set by Jesus when he said to many of those whom he had healed, "see that you tell no man of this." Today the motto is, "Tell everybody of this."

While undoubtedly many of the current professional faith healers are earnest men and women, there are also those who indulge in actual fraud. A notable instance of such fraud involved a highly publicized faith healer in Miami, Florida. Ten thousand people crowded into his tent every night to applaud what appeared to be remarkable healings. The most exciting incident of the whole series happened one night when a mother came with her little child of five or six years of age. The faith healer declared that the little girl was unable to utter a single word and that this was a tremendous handicap for her. The evangelist took the little girl on his knee and prayed over her. Then he spoke a word and told the child to repeat it. To the astonishment of everyone the child succeeded in doing this.

Then he uttered a second word and a third with similar success. The crowd, jamming the tent to its capacity, rose to its feet and cheered. A reporter of the Miami Herald was present and he made a point to seek out the mother of the child and secured her home address. The next day he asked her for the address of the school which the child attended. He looked up the principal who directed him to the speech teacher. He asked about the little girl in question and the speech teacher said, "Yes, it is a sad case and progress is bound to be very slow."

"You mean to say," asked the reported, "that this child cannot utter a single word?"

"Not quite that," said the teacher. "She has made a little progress. She can now say three words." And the teacher uttered the three words spoken by the evangelist, the words which all ten thousand persons in the great tent believed that the child had spoken for the first time that night.

The aftermath of some of these faith healing missions has been pitiful, with many disillusioned and despairing people finding that the temporary improvement produced by emotional excitement did not last. Undoubtedly, as in all such instances, there were cases of illness improved or cured. So great is the power of faith that it will produce results at times under the most unpromising conditions. But many of these "healings" have no element of permanence. It is true that our Lord healed people's physical and mental illness. Nowhere does he suggest that they should be passively accepted as the will of God. But he always put healings in a secondary position. His primary mission was to proclaim the Kingdom of God—the rule of God in the hearts of men and women. Apparently he regarded the public excitement over his healings as a hindrance to his primary task.

What makes the situation so confused and complicated is that these healing evangelists, however mistakenly, are concerned with a spiritual force that is undoubtedly real. Faith, especially if it is linked with God, releases energies that powerfully affect body, mind and spirit.

However, it is important to ask how we are to distinguish between a misuse of faith healing and a truly Christian employment of it. One of the sure earmarks of untrustworthiness in this field is the refusal of the 'healer' to submit any of his or her so called "cures" for medical examination. One competent investigator declares that he could not find one of the leading and much publicized "healers" who was willing to submit a case to a medical board.

The Christian Church must bear a measure of blame for the present situation. What has been one of the undoubted ministries of the church in apostolic days and at times since then, has been neglected or ignored, and most pastors have stubbornly refused to recognize the importance of spiritual healing. Consequently, the healing cults have moved into the vacuum thus created by the Church itself.

Medical science, too, must accept its share of responsibility. During the first part of the twentieth century many medical schools were dominated by a spirit of materialism. This point was stressed by Dr. A.B. Bond of Philadelphia who, in an address to ministers and doctors said, "When I went to medical school, …our anatomy teacher in his first lecture said, 'Man has a soul and a body. That's enough for the soul. For the next four years I shall be talking to you about the body.'" The physician added, "He lived up to his promise. We heard of nothing but the body." There were also those, of course, who would not even admit the existence of the soul; who believed man to be wholly a creature of his natural environment, living in a mechanistically determined universe. Today all this has largely changed. In an address to the New York Academy of Medicine a prominent physician referred to the spiritual element in man, and added, "There is something here, above and beyond the test tube which must come back into the relationship between the physician and patient." That "something here, above and beyond the test tube" is freely recognized today by the best—accredited medical science.

In their ministry to the sick, pastors see the work of physicians at close range, and often wonder if doctors themselves realize the tremendous psychological and spiritual impact made in the sick room by the personality of the physician, especially when he or she is a person of faith. Often we have seen the darkness of anxiety pass and the light of hope dawn on the faces of dear ones when the magical words are heard, "The doctor is here."

It is a mistake to differentiate, as some are now doing, between so called "divine healing" and medical healing. All healing is divine healing. Medical science and true faith healing are both of God. God is not more active in so called spiritual healing than he is in any other means of combating sickness. Physicians are truly God's agents of healing, whether or not they acknowledge this fact.

Little wonder that an ancient Hebrew Scripture declares that the physician is raised up of God for a divinely appointed task of healing: "Honor a physician according to thy need of him with the honors due unto him, for verily the Lord hath created him. For from the most High cometh healing." (Ecclesiastes 38: 1,2) At the same time we witness God's power at work in the prayer of faith.

Here is an actual happening. A pastor bows by the bedside of a parishioner whom he commends to the healing power of God. Medical science has despaired of saving the patient's life, but the quiet, even toned voice of the pastor quoting well loved passages from the Bible has had a strange and unlooked for result. The patient's breathing becomes normal. There are signs that he is coming out of a deep coma and returning to consciousness. His will to live is quickened and strengthened. In response to the spiritual

Spiritual Healing

therapy of Scriptures and prayers, healing forces of unpredictable power are at work drawing him back from the very gates of death. We are reminded of the familiar words of Dr. Alexis Carrel: "As a physician I have seen men, after all other therapy had failed, lifted out of disease and melancholy by the serene effort of prayer." One of the unfailing characteristics of the healing ministry of Jesus is that it was directed not to isolated human ills, but to the redemption of the whole individual. The entire personality was involved. A serious mistake is sometimes made by persons exercising a ministry of spiritual healing in that they are satisfied with the improvement or cure of an individual malady as an end in itself and unrelated to the character of the patient. A physical healing may sometimes be accomplished while spiritual ills remain—perhaps deeply rooted self-centeredness or even moral failure. But to be most effective, healing must be directed at the whole person. Luke, the Greek physician, gives us a typical illustration of Jesus' mode of healing. A woman creeps up behind him and touches the fringe of his garment. The medical men of her day regard her illness as a judgement of God. She is branded an outcast, expelled from the Temple, separated from her family, ostracized by society. But the doctors of that New Testament period were mistaken. Her illness was not produced by moral wrongdoing. Mark writes that she "suffered much under many physicians, and had spent all that she had, and was no better but rather grew worse." When Luke records the same incident, he is more generous in his treatment of the physicians, but then he himself was a doctor. Luke writes, "She had spent all her living upon physicians, neither could be healed of any."

When almost in the depths of despair, she hears of the Great Physician. His reputation as a healer has become known throughout the land. So the idea takes root in her mind that if she can but touch the hem of his robe she will be made whole. Resolving to put her hopes to the test, she joins the throng and works her way toward the Master. More than once, just as she is about to touch him, a surge of struggling humanity sweeps her back. Finally, with a desperate effort, she reaches out a thin, trembling hand and grasps the hem of his garment. When our Lord turns abruptly and asks, "Who touched me?" the disciples regard him with bewilderment. They point out that he has been thronged by hundreds of persons, so why does he ask such a question? He replies, "Someone touched me; for I perceive that power has gone forth from me."

The woman tries to hide herself because she knows that she has no right to be in that throng. The ban of the medical men and the church is on her. Now in fearfulness and trembling she confesses all to Jesus. His reply is full of reassurance. "Daughter," he says, calling her by that tender name which would indicate her restoration to God's family, "be of good comfort, your faith has made you whole; go in peace." Here was not merely the healing of a specific ailment, but the gift of "wholeness"—the redemption of an entire personality.

In the Academy of Medicine in New York, a prominent physician told a group of pastors and doctors that modern medicine had too long concentrated on a study of the disease to the neglect of the patient. Now, he said, we take into consideration the patient and also the environmental and emotional factors.

As an illustration of the manner in which spiritual influences could be a definite asset in a serious illness, he described a case history from his own clinic. He told of a plumber who had come in with a serious heart condition. He was given an electrocardiograph and x-ray examinations. As a result of the tests he was advised to give up his work immediately and to avoid all exertion. The prognosis was exceedingly discouraging, offering little more than a life of invalidism.

About a year later the physician received a report from one of the case workers at the clinic that this man was showing great improvement, that he was doing light work without adverse results, and shortly expected to resume a full time job. He was called in again, and the same series of tests were made. Said the lecturer: "To our amazement, we were unable to discover the slightest symptoms of the disease that seemed so marked twelve months earlier. I asked the man: 'What have you been doing in the last twelve months?' 'Well', he said, 'the future didn't look very bright to me. I followed your instructions, but since I had nothing else to do, I took up what I hadn't done for a long time. I began to read my Bible. As I read it, the peace of God came into my life, and little by little I found that I was improving. I have kept up the practice of Bible reading ever since.'"

"We discharged the man as cured," concluded the physician. At the time of the lecture the patient was carrying on his normal occupation.

This is not an isolated instance. I believe that as we draw to the end of the twentieth century one of the most important developments in both medicine and religion is the recognition of the healing power of faith, combined with medical science.

An article in our local newspaper of December 17, 1996 with a dateline from Boston declares: "Survey: Most doctors believe in link between faith and healing." It quotes Dr. Dale Matthews, a professor at Georgetown Medical School, as saying: "The spiritual traditions of healing will be joined with surgery and pharmaceuticals. I think we're entering the era of prayer and Prozac." It also reports on a study of prayer's effects on recovery from heart problems saying that the patients who received prayers had half as many complications as those who didn't. Of course, these studies simply bear out what Christians who believe in the power of prayer have known all along. It is good to know, however, that we can look forward to greater cooperation between religion, medicine, and psychology for the healing of God's children.

A young mother in the emergency room at Winston-Salem's North Carolina Baptist Hospital was sinking rapidly. Her baby had been killed in the auto accident, but her own injuries did not seem serious enough to be fatal. After the surgeon had done all he could, he called in a psychiatrist. "There's no medical reason why she shouldn't recover," he said, "but she wants to die—she will, unless her attitude is changed."

The psychiatrist's careful analysis uncovered the root of the woman's problem: the baby killed had been born as the result of an extramarital affair. She had been able to live with her secret as long as the child was alive, but now nothing the psychiatrist said could shake her guilt ridden interpretation of the accident's meaning. "I've got to die," she kept repeating. "It's God's punishment for my sin. I deserve it."

The psychiatrist summoned the chaplain. "This case calls for theological answers I haven't got." he said.

On several occasions the chaplain visited the patient, saying little, allowing her to express her remorse fully. When she was exhausted, he said quietly, "You say you must die. But isn't killing yourself—and that's what you are doing—just taking the easy way out? The selfish way? Your death will only bring what you feel is your judgement upon your fine husband and your other child. Do you think that's fair?"

During a long silence he let this sink in, then said softly, "'Wouldn't you like to use this tragedy to redeem your marriage and your life?"

Reassured and shown an avenue of hope, the woman cried, "Oh, I would, I would." And she did. Once she found a new purpose in living, her wounds healed rapidly. She has been an exemplary wife and mother ever since.

Theory and practice vary, but the testimony is the same: Healing often follows prayer and the act of faith. Why healings do not always come, or why they do not always seem permanent are questions impossible to answer. Yet we appear sometimes to experience eternity impinging upon time, to see the spiritual become manifest in the material, and so believe that grace supersedes law.

At other times when conditions appear to be similar, healings do not occur. All who practice spiritual healing experience 'failures' as well as 'successes'. But we are not to judge. Healing is not to be claimed as anyone's prerogative nor is it to be segmented. Healing and the healing of the whole person are the creative acts of God, no matter who the agent may be. He or she who has healing in their hands, be they physicians, surgeons, psychiatrists, pastors, or lay people, may only thank God humbly that they be used in this ministry.

The modern practice of comprehensive healing has been summarized as follows: The physician says, "Here is a body that is sick. I will address myself to that sickness, and with the latest drugs and surgical techniques I will make this body well."

The psychiatrist says: "Here is a mind with an anxiety that has made the patient physically and mentally ill. By analysis I will help this person gain insight into his or her problem, and by drawing upon their own resources they can help heal themselves."

The minister says: "Here is an immortal soul, whose sick body and disturbed mind have defeated this individual as a person. By giving him or her love and understanding, and by pointing them to resources outside themselves, I will help them to get beyond their body-mind disorders to their underlying causes: their sense of disharmony with themselves, their fellows, and their God."

Together all members of the healing team say: "Here is an individual who is body, mind and soul. This person's whole health is the sum of the health of the three. Only by working together, each in his or her own specialty, can we heal the whole person."

It is significant that not over a church door, but over the entrance of one of America's greatest medical centers is engraved the legend: "For from the Most High Cometh Healing."

Chapter 13

The Kingdom Of God

There is nothing in Christian Theology about which there is more disagreement among serious minded students than the meaning of the Kingdom of God. All agree that it was the central message of Jesus. If we open the New Testament to almost any place in the first three Gospels, we find parables of the Kingdom and other references to its coming. We should expect, therefore, that it would be easy enough to discover what he was talking about. However, there are so many recorded sayings about the Kingdom, some of them apparently contradictory that various theories have been developed as to what Jesus really meant by it, and what we should mean.

It will not be useful to go into all the fine distinctions as to these theories. One view, held by the premilleniests, puts the emphasis on the physical second coming of Christ, and holds that the Kingdom will come when Christ returns. Another view agrees with this in holding that the Kingdom will come only when God intervenes to put an end to the course of history as we know it, but it puts the Kingdom wholly in another world instead of on earth. Both of these positions get their authority from the apocalyptic passages in the New Testament, which seem to predict the end of this earthly scheme of things by a sudden, dramatic act of God.

A very different view centers in Jesus' saying, "The Kingdom of God is within you." It regards the Kingdom as already present in the lives of redeemed individuals to whom Christ has come with transforming power. People who hold this view do not usually look for a physical second coming, but believe that Christ comes to people in Spirit, as God's greatest gift, whenever they will receive him. This has been stated admirably in Philips Brooks' Christmas hymn:

*"How silently, how silently
The wondrous gift is given.
So God imparts to human hearts
The blessings of his heaven.
No ear may hear his coming,
But in this world of sin,
Where meek souls will receive him still,
The dear Christ enters in."*

Still another view of the Kingdom is that of a Christianized society in which justice and love will prevail—a Kingdom not yet achieved, but which people must work for with great earnestness. The Kingdom thus becomes the main incentive to a social gospel. This too, may be typified by the words of a hymn:

*"Rise up O men of God,
His Kingdom tarries long;
Bring in the day of brotherhood
And end the night of wrong."*

This social interpretation of the Kingdom, which scarcely anyone held before the nineteenth century, has been so widely advocated, particularly in America, that by many it is regarded as THE doctrine of the Kingdom.

What shall we make of these views? The last two can be combined, for both look at the coming of the Kingdom as a gradual process taking place here on earth. The salvation of the individual and of society need not—in fact, must not—be separated, and in both humanity has a definite responsibility. The first two views are on a very different basis, for they despair of the salvation of this world and hold that God, in his own good time, will do whatever needs to be done about bringing in the next.

Probably Jesus shared with others of his time the apocalyptic expectation of a speedy end of the world. Most biblical scholars believe that he did. However, if one takes his message as a whole, it is clear that his main emphasis lies elsewhere. The note he was always urging was the need of dependence on God and obedience to God in all the relations of life, that God's Kingdom might come and his will be done on earth as it is in heaven.

The central meaning of The Kingdom is the righteous, loving rule of God. God demands allegiance like a king; he loves us like a father. If one takes the rule of God as the keynote, many otherwise contradictory passages can be harmonized. The rule of God is already present, yet it must come in the fullness of time when people repent and seek to do God's will on earth. It comes in this world, but the final victory of God's rule lies, not on earth, but in a realm beyond this world. It grows gradually and almost imperceptibly, like a leaven or mustard seed; it comes suddenly, like a thief in the night, or the bridegroom at a wedding, and one must be ready and on the watch. "It is the Father's good pleasure to give you the Kingdom," yet he gives it to the one who, prizing it like a pearl of great price or a treasure hid in the field, gives for it all that they have.

Not all the things that have been believed by Christians about the Kingdom can be reconciled, but the heart of them can be. This was done at the world missionary conference in Madras in words that are worth quoting: "The Kingdom of God is both present and future; both a growth and a final consummation by God. It is our task and our hope—our task which we face with the power of Christ; our hope that the last word will be spoken by God and that that last word will be victory. The Kingdom means both acceptance and action, a gift and a task. We work for it and we wait for it."

Whether the social meaning of the Kingdom is a right interpretation depends on whether we base our judgement on what Jesus directly said and did. There is little doubt that he was mainly concerned with individuals rather than with social systems. Though he says much in condemnation of selfishness, greed, hypocrisy, and the like, there is no direct word in his recorded sayings about slavery, war, or the political oppression rampant in his day. But this does not mean that no social application can be drawn from his words. Everywhere and always he believed in persons, and whatever people might think, he always treated them with the love and respect due a child of God. To the extent that we take seriously these two factors, the righteous rule of God and Jesus' estimate of persons, we are bound to do all we can to remove barriers that cripple and warp and hamper our brothers and sisters in the family of God. Only so can God's Kingdom come and his will be done on earth.

The social gospel is justified, not in the sense that by it we ourselves can build the Kingdom, but in the obligation to be God's servants in removing obstacles to the abundant life he waits to give. As long as poverty, ignorance, disease, race prejudice, exploitation, oppression, and war remain, God's will for persons cannot be fully done. The best analogy for our relation to the Kingdom is not that of a builder, but the sower of whom Jesus spoke in one of his greatest parables. It is our job to sow the seed and if possible remove the rocks and thorns that choke it; it is God who brings forth the fruit from the ground, some thirty, some sixty, some a hundredfold.

We come now to the question which in some respects is the hardest of all, but which nobody who tries seriously to be a Christian can evade. How can we know the will of God? And if we know it, can we do it?

As to how to know the will of God, two warnings are necessary at the outset. First, we must not be so sure we know it that we shall be intolerant of equally sincere Christians who think differently. Second, we must be sure enough that we know it to go ahead with confidence. As in all search for truth, we must combine open mindedness and a teachable spirit with convictions to live by. The combination is not easy, but it is essential if we are not to be bigoted or to flounder in uncertainties.

If we are to know the will of God in a decision we have to make, such as what vocation to choose, how to deal with a difficult person, what to do about war, several things are necessary. They are not easy. Briefly stated, they are these: (1) We must learn the mind of Christ. (2) We must let ourselves be led by the Holy Spirit. (3) We must view the situation in its total setting, and particularly the consequences. (4) We must act by the light we have.

In order to "let this mind be in you, which was also in Christ Jesus," as Paul put it, it is necessary to live with the New Testament until it becomes a part of us. There is no single passage, not even such great ones as the Sermon on the Mount or the magnificent hymn of love in the thirteenth chapter of First Corinthians, that says it all. There is no rule, not even the Golden Rule, that can be applied automatically. Yet there is a spirit of devotion to God and love for people, pervading the accounts of the life and words and works of Jesus, that is the indispensable basis of any Christian action.

In the second place, we must pray and be open to the leading of the Holy Spirit. The Holy Spirit, or the Spirit of God, is that continuing, indwelling presence of God which we could be aware of at all times if we were not too dull to sense this presence. When we pray, if we pray humbly and receptively as we should, we let down the barriers and listen to the voice of God. The answer comes, sometimes in overwhelming clear convictions, sometimes in dim intuitions of the direction in which to move. Such answers can be taken as God's leading only if we are careful to make God's will, and not our own wishes, determine the current of our praying. Often we are left with a great deal of thinking yet to do.

In the third place (not third in time, for all these steps should proceed together), we must look as clearly, as widely, and as fair mindedly as we can at the situation. Here the help of a trusted counselor, one's pastor, family, or friends, is often very valuable. Nobody can decide the question for us, but often somebody else can point out the consequences we have not seen or thought about. It is essential that one ask which of the possible courses of action will do the most good, not to oneself only, but to all the persons who may be affected by it. One has to reckon with the fact that to do the most Christlike thing may bring suffering to oneself and to those one loves. One ought not to shrink from a cross, but neither ought one to court martyrdom simply for the sake of feeling noble.

Finally, having made as Christian a decision as is possible under the circumstances, one must go ahead by the light one has, while awaiting more. "If any man willeth to do his will, he shall know of the teaching, whether it is of God." without such decision life grows flabby and lacks the purpose that spiritual health and wholeness requires. God may continue to prick the conscience when we do wrong, but before long a vision disregarded fades away.

But, having discovered what we sincerely believe to be the will of God for us in our time and place and circumstances, can we do it? The answer is both yes and no. We can set our faces toward the right, pray for God's help as we go forward, and accomplish much. This must be said in reply to those who believe that, because Christianity demands an impossible perfection, it is a beautiful but impractical ideal. For the past two thousand years people who have tried to do the will of God as revealed in Christ have made a great difference in the world, both through the strength and radiance of their own lives and their impact on their times. Most of the morally and spiritually constructive movements of history have stemmed from this source. There is no reason now to give up trying.

On the other hand, it is a mistake to suppose that any of us will ever do perfectly the will of God. In the most dedicated Christian, there are always enough roots of self-love to keep one humble and in need of continual repentance. There have been, and there still are, Christian saints; but no real saint ever thinks of themselves as one because they know too well their need of God's forgiveness. The most effective Christian life is that of the person who, distrusting their own righteousness, trusts God enough to go forward in spite of their limitations.

Must every moral decision involve choosing "the lesser of two evils"? Many believe so, and in a sense it is true, for life comes mixed with evil elements. But if we turn the phrase around, we shall have something that in reality is much truer. Every choice is between a greater and a lesser good, and we ought to choose the greater. The difference between this and "the lesser of two evils" lies in the fact that the greater good means the more Christlike action. We have then, not merely to choose between conflicting evils. The more important fact is that in these choices, we must and can, have a perfect goal to steer by and a perfect source of power to draw upon. This is far more than a verbal difference. Whether we believe that Christianity can save the world in its present tangle of evil forces depends much on the degree to which we keep the goal in view and try humbly to draw upon this power.

Immanuel Kant once said that all human behavior, all ethics, boils down to a single point: acting "as if" certain things were true. Christians are called upon to act "as if" the Kingdom of God is a reality; "as if" God really does govern the world. When Jesus said, "The kingdom of God is within you," he was trying to tell us that we are to live as members of the Kingdom now; we are to let Christ rule in our lives. In that way we can be part of the solution to the world's ills rather than part of the problem. John Killinger tells the story of a woman in the South whose club was voting on the admission of its first black member. The woman knew that if she voted her conscience it could well mean she would be ostracized and her husband's medical practice could be jeapordized. On the other hand she could not reconcile her Christian conviction with the social practice of segregation. When the day came for the vote to her own surprise she found herself making a speech to her fellow club members about the Kingdom of God.

In spite of her speech, or maybe because of it, the black woman was not accepted into membership, and this woman found herself excluded from future luncheons and committees.

Several years later six women who had belonged to the same club came to her and asked if she would join them in starting a new club that would be open to women of all races. Here was a woman who stood up for her belief in the Kingdom, and eventually because of this the Kingdom became more of a reality for those around her.

Jesus said: "Seek first the Kingdom of God, and everything else will be yours as well." Remember the Kingdom of God is like leaven which a woman took and hid in three measures of flour until it was all leavened.

Chapter 14

You Must Forgive To Be Forgiven

The only persons to whom this chapter is addressed are those conscious of moral wrongdoing. If you have no uneasy stirrings of conscience about your attitude toward anything or your relationship with anybody, then this chapter is not for you. For we are going to be dealing with the forgiveness of sins.

If you have read this far and have about decided to skip this chapter because you are sure that you do not come within range of this subject's interest and scope let me suggest that first you be sure you understand what we mean by 'sin'. So often when we use that word we have in the background of our minds a specific list of gross iniquities—murder, robbery, sensuality, drunkenness, Those plainly are sins. But before any person endeavors to avoid his or her share in the need of forgiveness, let them add at least three categories more to that carnal list.

Let them add sins of temperament—sullenness, vindictiveness, peevishness, jealousy, bad temper. How much more prevalent they are; how much more harm they do; how much more hidden evil they reveal than even passionate sins. In Jesus' greatest Parable, which we call The Prodigal Son, the Prodigal represents sins of passion, and ruinous as they are, he did come home again. But the Elder Brother represents sins of temper. With the Prodigal home, the house alight, music playing, dancing in full swing, it is written of the Elder Brother that "he was angry, and would not go in." Bad temper, sullen, envious, bitter—that, as Jesus saw it, keeps some people from the Father's house more hopelessly than sins of passion do.

If anyone seeks to avoid his or her share in the need of forgiveness, let them add also sins of social attitude. There are many great and small rogues today who do evil for political and economic organizations that they never would think of doing for themselves.

Nor should anyone try to escape his or her share in the need of forgiveness until they have added to the list sins of neglect. It is not alone the things we do; it is the things we leave undone that haunt us—the letters we did not write, the words we did not speak, the opportunity we did not take. How insistently Jesus stressed the importance of this type of evil. What was the matter with the man who hid his one talent? What did he do? That was the trouble—he did nothing; he missed his chance. What was the trouble with the priest and the Levite who left the victim on the road? What did they do? That was the difficulty—they did nothing; they went on the other side and did nothing.

Are you still wondering if this chapter is meant for you? Well, let me put it this way. Hayes Jones was twenty-six years old in 1964 when the Olympics were held in Tokyo. Hayes Jones ran a specialty; he leaped over the high hurdles in a 110 meter dash in thirteen and six-tenths seconds to win a gold medal. All the time he was training for the Olympics he was working to remove the six-tenths of a second hoping to win the high hurdles in Tokyo in thirteen seconds flat. Whatever is represented by that six-tenths of a second, I suggest is an encumbrance, or in the nature of our meaning of sin. Four years later Willie Davenport won that race in thirteen and three-tenths seconds; and in 1980 the winner did it in under thirteen seconds.

Sin is anything that adds burdensome weight to life or takes away tone of muscle, mind, or personality. Sin is that over indulgence of anything that will add six-tenths of a second to the man who wants to be able to fly over high hurdles with an almost unbroken rhythm of running.

Or let us describe it another way. There was a young nineteen year-old girl in Vermont named Marsha Fletcher. She had her eye on a skiing championship. One day she came down the national trail in one minute and forty-two seconds and won the event eight-tenths of a second over another young girl.

I do not have that kind of a watch which can measure the split seconds of those differentials between one young lady whisking down the slope in a snow storm to win, and the other tearful competitor coming in eight-tenths of a second later to be the loser. But this distinction is what we are trying to say is like unto the meaning of sin.

In the Epistle to the Hebrews, it is said that we should lay aside the weight and the sin that does so easily obstruct us. Anything that obstructs love, life, faith, hope, unity and personality becomes sin. So the need to be forgiven is caused by anything that hinders us from living at our best.

There was a day in World War II when the B-17 bombers were so important to us that in the urgency of the advance they were stripped of their olive drab paint. It was found that at least thirty-seven pounds of paint could be removed from the burden of that aircraft and thus extend its range. That is what I mean by sin being a burden or an obstruction to a fuller life.

We are so impatient with people. We are not adulterers, murderers, liars, or thieves, but we are cruel, harsh, impatient and unforgiving. We judge other people, and ourselves as well. This is our sin. This attitude is the six-tenths of a second or the differential that would spoil our victory. But forgiveness is the divine reconciliation. Forgiveness is the grace of God which declares that a fault can be eliminated in our pursuit of excellence in the high hurdle race of existence.

How do we get this forgiveness? First of all, we have to forgive ourselves. After that we have to forgive other people. Then we have to forgive God for making us, and the

This I Believe

universe, operate the way we do. Then you will find that God always stands ready to forgive us if we will repent of our sins and accept his forgiveness.

To forgive yourself is not easy. This is the thing people are not doing enough. They talk about the religious language of forgiveness, but they are not forgiving themselves. Look again at Jesus' incomparable story of the Prodigal Son. Before the boy knew anything of his father's forgiveness, when he was in the pigsty breaking his cultural pattern, violating his integrity and ideology, he took a stick and broke it on the head of one of the swine and muttered, "I will go to my father and say, 'Father I have sinned. Make me as one of your hired servants.'" He had already forgiven himself the moment he started back home, but what he did not know was that all during this time he had been forgiven by his father who waited for him to come to his senses and return home.

Put it another way. One of the religious atheists of our time, Albert Camus who died in an automobile accident, in his novel, The Fall, describes his own introspection. The main character had a minor automobile accident. He jumped out of his car and found himself ready to punch the man in the other car. That night he wrote, "How ashamed I am of my viciousness. Why did I feel that way?" Later in the year his sweetheart left him. He was angry and asked himself the reason. "I wanted her only for myself," was the answer. He was amazed at his vanity. Later in his despondency, while walking across the bridge over the Seine, he heard a cry for help in the dark swirling waters. He ran and looked over the railing. He could see no one. He was tempted, for a moment, to leap to the rescue, but then he reconsidered prudently. All the rest of the night he thought, "Yes, and I am a coward also."

We need to forgive ourselves for our vanity, our cowardice, our viciousness, because Jesus Christ taught us that God forgives us these very things. He came so we could find forgiveness and humility, as in "The Fool's Prayer" by Edward Rowland Sill.

"The royal feast was done; the King
Sought some new sport to banish care,
And to his jester cried: 'Sir Fool,
Kneel now, and make for us a prayer!'

The jester doffed his cap and bells,
And stood the mocking court before;
They could not see the bitter smile
Behind the painted grin he wore.

He bowed his head, and bent his knee
Upon the monarch's silken stool;
His pleading voice arose: 'O Lord,
Be merciful to me, a fool!'

The room was hushed; in silence rose
The King, and sought his garden cool,
And walked apart, and murmured low,
'Be merciful to me, a fool!'"

We need to forgive ourselves, always remembering though that this means more than murmuring, "I'm sorry." We must truly repent of our sins and determine to lead a new life, following henceforth the commandments of God.

A man sought counsel and asked, "Why am I so nervous?" It developed later that he was the administrator of his father's estate bequeathed to him and his brother. He was not being honest with his brother. It was only when he made restitution that his life was changed. Forgiveness provides our lives with direction and responsibility.

We also need to forgive other people. Doctors say that much of our illness is associated with our unforgiven relationships with other people. In one clinical case a woman with a fractured hip was not responding at all. The second doctor on the case asked her, "What is bothering you?"

She replied, "I can't forgive the first doctor." But when she did, her chart showed a change for the better.

The only difficulty with talking about the necessity of forgiving others is that inevitably it leads to the fact that the Bible teaches us to love our neighbors as ourselves, and because in Christian morals "neighbors" includes our "enemies," we come up against this terrible duty of forgiving our enemies.

Everyone says forgiveness is a lovely idea, until they have something to forgive, as we did say at the end of the Vietnam War or World War II. And then, to mention the subject at all is to be greeted with howls of anger. It is not that people think this too high and difficult a virtue: it is that they think it hateful and contemptible. 'That sort of talk makes me sick', they say. And some would respond by saying, 'How would you feel about forgiving the Gestapo if you were a Jew?'

Well, I wonder how I would feel. Just as when Christianity tells me that I must not deny my religion even to save myself from death by torture. I wonder very much what I would do when it came to that point. But I am not telling or trying to tell you what I could do—I can do precious little—I am telling you what Christianity is. I did not invent it. And there, right in the middle of it, I find "Forgive us our sins as we forgive those who sin against us." There is not the slightest suggestion that we are offered forgiveness on any other terms. It is made perfectly clear that if we do not forgive we shall not be forgiven. There are no two ways about it.

What are we to do? It is going to be hard enough anyway, but I think there are two things we can do to make it easier. When you start mathematics you do not begin with the calculus, you begin with simple addition. In the same way, if we really want to learn how to forgive, perhaps we had better start with something easier than the Gestapo. One might start with forgiving one's husband or wife, or parents, or children for something they have done or said in the last week. That will probably keep us busy for the moment. And secondly, we might try to understand exactly what loving your neighbor as yourself means. Well, how exactly do I love myself?

Now that I come to think about it, I don't exactly have a feeling of fondness or affection for myself, and I don't even always enjoy my own society. So apparently "Love your neighbor" does not mean "feel fond of him or her," or "find him or her attractive." I ought to have seen that before, because, of course, you cannot feel fond of a person by trying. Do I think well of myself, think myself a nice fellow? Well, I am afraid I sometimes do (and those are, no doubt, my worst moments), but that is not why I love myself. In fact, it is the other way around: my self-love makes me think myself nice, but thinking myself nice is not why I love myself. So loving my enemies does not apparently mean thinking them nice either. That is an enormous relief. For a good many people imagine that forgiving your enemies means making out that they are not really such bad fellows after all, when it is quite plain that they are. Go a step further. In my most clearsighted moments not only do I not think myself a nice person, but I know that I am a miserable creature. I can look at some of the things I have done with loathing. So apparently I am allowed to loathe and hate some of the things my enemies do. Now that I come to think of it, I remember Christian teachers telling me long ago that I must hate a person's bad actions, but not hate the bad person: or as they would say, hate the sin but not the sinner.

For a long time I used to think this a silly, straw-splitting distinction: how could you hate what a person did and not hate the person? But years later it occurred to me that there was one person to whom I had been doing this all my life—namely myself. However much I might dislike my own cowardice, or conceit, or greed, or ill temper I went on loving myself. There had never been the slightest difficulty about it. In fact, the very reason why I hated the things was that I loved the man. Just because I loved myself, I was sorry to find that I was the sort of person who did these things. Consequently, Christianity does not want us to reduce by one iota the hatred we feel for cruelty and treachery. We ought to hate them. But we want to hate them in the same way in which we hate things in ourselves: being sorry that the person should have done such things, and hoping, if it is anyway possible, that somehow, somewhere, that person can be cured and made human again.

The real test is this. Suppose one reads a story of atrocities in the paper. Be they Iranian, Chinese, Libyan, Bosnian, or some 'hoods' here in our own country. Then suppose that something turns up suggesting that the story might not be quite true, or not quite so bad as it was first made out. Is one's feeling, "Thank God," or is it a feeling of disappointment, and even a determination to cling to the first story for the sheer pleasure of thinking your enemies as bad as possible? If it is the latter, then it is, I am afraid, the first step in a process which, if followed to the end, will make us into devils. You see, one is I beginning to wish that evil was a little more evil. If we give that wish its head, later on we shall insist on seeing everything—God and ourselves and our friends all included—as bad, and not be able to stop doing it: we shall be fixed for ever in a universe of pure hatred.

I admit that what we have been saying means that we are called upon to love people who have nothing lovable about them. Perhaps it makes it easier if we remember that that is how God loves us. Not for any nice, attractive qualities we think we have, but just because we are the things called 'selves'. For really there is nothing else in us to love: creatures like us who actually find hatred such a pleasure that to give it up is like giving up candy or our favorite dessert.

We may not completely understand just what happens in the experience of God's forgiveness, but there are two things about it of which we can be quite sure. The first is that to know that we are forgiven is to enter into a new and richer dimension of life. The second is that we can never know the grace of being forgiven except as we also know that of forgiving. To refuse to forgive is precisely to hug the past, to cling to it, to refuse to give it up. To forgive and to be forgiven are two sides of the same shield. We can have neither without the other.

We must always keep in mind that our heavenly Father yearns for us to come home; to turn from our sinful ways, and accept his forgiveness so that we might live in harmony with him. So too, with those who have sinned against us; we should yearn for them to come to their senses, repent of their wrongdoings, and come seeking the forgiveness which we are as eagerly waiting to give them as is our heavenly Father.

In the Church of St. Mary Woolnoth, in the city of London, there is an inscription which reads:

"John Newton, Clerk,
Once an infidel and libertine;
A servant of slaves in Africa:
Was by the rich mercy of our
Lord and Saviour Jesus Christ,
Preserved, restored, and pardoned,
And appointed to preach the Faith
He had long laboured to destroy.
Near sixteen years at Olney in Bucks,
And twenty-seven years in this church."

That inscription sums up the life of the man who wrote "Amazing Grace." At the age of eleven, John Newton, son of a master mariner, was a sailor on his father's ship...a happy-go-lucky boy. He lost his ship, and when he was a midshipman in the navy he lost his ship again and was publicly flogged and degraded for the offense. He managed to get to the African Coast and eventually became a master of a slave ship. However, through his study of the Scripture he finally came to realize that this trafficking in human lives was un-Christian. And so at forty he decided to become an evangelical clergyman. If ever there was a twice-born man, it was John Newton. He was certain of his faith because he knew at first hand the transforming power of the Gospel. It was out of his own experience that he wrote:

*"Amazing Grace! how sweet the sound
That saved a wretch like me!
I once was lost, but now am found,
Was blind, but now I see."*

John Newton knew at first hand what it meant to be forgiven, and his life was never the same after he accepted the love of Christ.

One last word needs to be said if we are to understand 'forgiveness.' There are often dire consequences that result from our wrong doing. Our mistakes, our bad decisions, our careless ways, may do harm to ourselves, our loved ones, or others. To be forgiven does not imply that there are no penalties to be paid. We are responsible for our actions. To be forgiven in the sense we have been talking about means that we do not have to bear the burden of a guilty conscience, but we may be called upon to pay for our misdeeds. To forgive does not mean that every repentant criminal should be released from prison, nor that those accused of "War Crimes" should not be tried and if convicted, sentenced. Let there be no mistake about it. To forgive and to be forgiven is not to let us off the hook, to find an escape from the consequences of sin. Rather it is the only means by which we can restore a right relationship between God and ourselves, between our neighbor and ourselves, and thus be able to live life to the fullest as God intended it.

"If you forgive men their trespasses, your heavenly Father will also forgive you; but if you do not forgive men their trespasses neither will your Father forgive your trespasses." (Mark 11:25)

This I Believe

Chapter 15

What About Judgement?

There was a day when 'Judgement' and 'Damnation' were favorite topics for preachers who literally tried to scare the 'hell' out of their parishioners by painting vivid and terrifying pictures of the fiery furnaces of hell which awaited them unless they repented. The lurid descriptions of hell painted by preachers like Jonathan Edward often moved his hearers to moan and shriek and hurl themselves to the floor.

Likewise, artists of another day reveled in depicting the scene of "The Last Judgement," or in writings such as Dante's "Inferno." But today you rarely here a sermon on the subject. It is just not considered proper or fashionable. On the other hand, if we read the Gospels we are amazed to find how many times Jesus talked about Judgement and condemnation. In fact, we find that Jesus was simply carrying to its fulfillment the Old Testament teachings where people, cities, or lands that did not surrender to the righteousness of God would be destroyed.

There can be no doubt about it. We are expected to be righteous as God is righteous, and if we fall short we are liable to judgement. However, God does not really want to punish those who are not perfect as he is perfect. What he really wants most of all is to make peace with us when we fall short, and reconcile us to himself. This is Jesus' message!

It is a marvelous thing that, through the ages, we have kept our eyes fastened on a small, first century village in Palestine, and have instinctively asked, in any thought or undertaking: "What would Jesus think of this?" Life has taken on depth of meaning because the character of Christ and his thought and deeds have become the basic standard for judgement on the part of the human race.

The biblical record reflects the fact that one finds the moral imperative of God's righteous judgement merely by coming into the presence of Jesus. Zacchaeus, a money grabbing materialist, stands before the Master for a few moments and finds the whole structure of his values being swept away by the moral challenge of Jesus. And he builds then and there a new life in Christ. A woman, about to be lynched because of adultery, is saved by Jesus who utters no word of condemnation. But her accusers slink away because they cannot meet the simple standard that Jesus sets for their action. "Let the one among you who is without sin be the first one to throw a stone." Later, he says quietly: "I do not condemn you, but go and sin no more." She is self-condemned for her sordid life as she finds herself in the presence of the moral purity of the Master.

Yet, Jesus' word: "And this is the judgement, that the light has come into the world, and men loved darkness rather than light, because their deeds were evil." (John 3:19) points to our problem, and in so doing, gives us light on what he thought about judgement.

Jesus saw that judgement comes as a consequence of God's righteousness, as a consequence of people choosing to sin rather than not to sin, and that the judgement has come because God has come in Christ and brought the light that shows up the shabbiness of the dark corners of the human heart.

We need to understand that Jesus saw clearly that judgement is an inevitable implication of the fact that God is a righteous God who has created a moral universe. Georgia Harkness has commented on this in "The Gospel and Our World" in these words:

"Judgement implies condemnation—a God of sternness, even severity, who cannot be complacent before sin. It means dynamic opposition to injustice and evil, terrible in

What About Judgement?

the power of righteous indignation joined with righteous love. But at its center is a loving God 'whose mercy endureth forever', and who, because he desires righteousness in his erring children; works both in the lives of individuals and the currents of history to win men to obedience."

Jesus revealed that in God we have "an irreconcilable hostility to all evil, an irrevocable antagonism to sin." The biblical writers made much of the "wrath of God." Too often, I think, we have assumed that the kind of hostility God has toward evil demands an angry kind of God who vents his personal malice and vindictiveness on all evil and on the evildoer as well.

Stephen Neill points out that this is not true to the real nature of God as revealed to us in Jesus Christ. "His wrath is no more than the clear shining of his light, which must go forth implacably to the destruction of all darkness."

One recalls the movie scene where prisoners are seeking escape from their prison, and the terrifying beams of the spotlights are being moved along the walls with pitiless penetration to the farthest corners of darkness. In the movie, "The Spy Who Came In From The Cold", the final scene is dramatically done in this fashion. The spotlights on the east side of the Berlin Wall played a strategic role in putting the escaping hero and heroine in the pitiless center of the spotlight so the merciless machine guns can do their grim reaping. When we find ourselves in the spotlight of that great white light which has come from God, we are aware of his hostility toward all forms of evil and his antagonism for all sin.

God is not neutral in the constant war against sin and evil. To live in a world where God didn't care would be a nightmare. It is only the doctrine of the wrath of God, of his irreconcilable hostility to all evil, that makes life tolerable in such a world as ours.

Judgement is a consequence of this divine hostility to all evil. "The wrath of God is revealed from heaven against all ungodliness and wickedness of men," warned Paul in his word to Roman Christians. He was pointing not to a petulant deity so much as to the actual state of affairs in human life as the appalling results of human sin.

The coming of Jesus revealed not only the sin of man through the obvious comparison of Christ's light and man's darkness, but also it was a revelation of the heart of God "which utterly condemns evil but loves the evildoer—even when he is doing evil." In Jesus as the revealer of God's righteousness, we do indeed see God at work, exposing evil for what it is; yet, at the same time, we see him revealing himself as a God of mercy, forgiveness, and reconciliation.

Jesus' words about men loving darkness rather than the light which has come into the world are an indictment of our persistence in choosing darkness even when we have the chance for light. We choose the darkness of hate when love is offered as light for life.

One tragically recalls man's fatal choice on that significant day when Jesus was on trial before Pilate. Here was God's love revealed in all its redeeming power. Yet man chose Barabbas rather than Jesus, the zealot purveyor of hatred toward the enemy, rather than the Nazarene who spoke about loving your enemies.

It is so often easier to think ill of another person than to love him. Let's face it, all of us at times are transparently unlovable. And, the wonder is not that people cannot stand us, but that people do, indeed, tolerate us! If we sit in the circle of antagonistic dislike or hatred for another, we can build ourselves up by tearing the other fellow down.

Why do men love darkness when the light of love is offered by God in Christ?

Again we choose the darkness of self-sufficiency when only the savior of the world is strong enough to save us.

What About Judgement?

Here is the light of life come into our world to save us. The light is here. We have the power to apprehend it. It is ours for the accepting. But we skirt around its fringes, fearful of coming out of the darkness where we have learned to live and to find what little security is to be found there. The light hurts our eyes and we shut them quickly against the strain and the pain.

After you have watched a movie in a darkened theatre, the house lights are turned on and it takes a while to adjust your eyes to the brightness. Suppose you refused to do this. You just keep them closed in an effort to prevent the unpleasant feeling of the brightness hitting your eyes which have become comfortably accustomed to the darkness.

Silly, one would say. Yet, Jesus pointed out that this is exactly what we do when we depend on ourselves alone to get through the difficult journey of life. There is light for our journey, but we choose to depend on our means of getting along in the darkness of our own self-sufficiency.

All of this suggests that we seem to prefer the darkness of a selfmade hell when the light of heaven is all around us.

What makes hell? Certainly not physical torture inflicted by an angry God of vengeance. Certainly not the external conditions of a place reserved in the hereafter to torture the damned. Dr. Rall suggests that some of the elements involved in hell are: "...separation from that God who is light and life and peace; the fact that we must inescapably live with ourselves, that our world is the evil world of self which we have made. Sin is selfishness. The consequences of sin is not only that man is shut up with himself, but also that he is shut out, by his own choice, from others. This too, is hell, just as high and enriching fellowship makes heaven. Thus hell means death, just as faith and love mean life as they join us to God and our brothers. And this hell has a tragic existence here on earth."

Christ has illuminated all our values, and in his light we judge ourselves. Shortly before the Last Supper, Jesus declared: "He who believes in me, believes not in me but in him who sent me. I have come as light into the world, that whoever believes in me may not remain in darkness. If anyone hears my sayings and does not keep them, I do not judge him; for I did not come to judge the world but to save the world. He who rejects me and does not receive my sayings has a judge; the word that I have spoken will be his judge on the last day." (John 12:44-48)

The coming of Christ set a new standard for human judgement. He brought a new light that made our darkness even more of a contrast to the light. In that light we could see what men before could not see—the contrasting sins and evil. You can illustrate this by going into a room that has been closed up for awhile. If it is night and darkness is around, you cannot see the dust that has silently gathered during the room's isolation. But turn on the lights, or open the shades, and the dust is evident on tables, chairs, and floors. Dust shows in the light, but not in the darkness. Christ has so illuminated our values that, in his light, we find the basis for judging ourselves in a way that was not possible before. Leslie Weatherhead wrote in, "When The Lamp Flickers": "The highest court of justice is in the heart of a man just after the light of Christ has illuminated his motives and all his inner life."

Judgement, then, would seem to be based on how much we are growing toward the light. What are we doing with the light that has been given to us? Our judgement is not based on comparison to what the other fellow does with his gift of the light of God in Christ. Rather we are judged only on the basis of what we do with what we have been given by God.

Jesus' thought in this regard is found in the Parable of the Talents. Three men are entrusted with varying amounts of money or endowment by their employer, based on his judgement of their capabilities. On his return, he calls them in for an accounting. Two of the three have made good use of their trust, but the third has kept his talent buried in darkness, unwilling to use it because it seemed so small in comparison to the others. Jesus pointed out that the third man's judgement was negative, not because he was only a one talent man while the others were five talent and ten talent men, but because he refused to grow toward the light which had been revealed to him by using well his gifts.

It boils down to what Studdert-Kennedy, a British chaplain, said about the Judgement Day. He said he believed there would be just one question asked on that day when he appeared before his Maker. God would say to him: "What did you make of it?" And that is what each day's close—as judgement day—asks of each of us: "This gift of life which I, your heavenly Father have given you what did you make of it?"

"And this is the judgement, that the light has come into the world, and men loved darkness rather than light."

John Killinger sums it up when he says: "Judgement and reconciliation. They are at the heart of the gospel. They are what Christ's teachings were all about. Whether we believe in judgement now or judgement later, we know that it is an inescapable fact of life; and the good news of Christ is that God wants us to be rejoined with him and to be whole again!"

This I Believe

Chapter 16

Dealing With The Devil

Night has fallen on the little farm and the tired owner is going to bed. Before settling down to rest his aching limbs, he has one last look out the window. A thin moon gives just enough light to let him see the field in which he and his men have been sowing since dawn. He gives a sigh of contentment. The soil was just right; the seed was good; now they just have to wait until the first shoots of the wheat break through. He turns in and is soon asleep.

So there is no one to see a shadowy stranger who reaches the field a few hours later with a basket in his hands. With a stealthy speed he covers the field scattering seed, and just before the first streaks of dawn he slips away over the horizon to a distant farm.

Some weeks later the farmer wakes with the light and looks out. With a thrill he sees that the field is mottled with the first stirrings of his crop. He goes out to meet his servants and they rejoice in the hope of an unusually good harvest. A few days later his hopes are dashed as a servant wakes him with the news that right across the field weeds are sprouting with the wheat. He is horrified when he identifies it as the poisonous darnel, a bearded plant that grows to be about the same height as wheat. The servants immediately ask the question that gardeners have asked from prehistoric times to today, "Where did the weeds come from?" In this case the answer comes swiftly: "It was some enemy who did this."

The servants can't wait to deal with the situation. It is obvious to them that it requires immediate action.

"Do you want us to go and pull up the weeds?" The farmer has more sense. "No," he answers, "because as you gather up the weeds you might pull up some of the wheat along with them. Let the wheat and the weeds both grow together until harvest. Then I will tell the harvest workers to pull up the weeds first, tie them in bundles and burn them, and then gather in the wheat and put it in my barn."

This is the story that Jesus told, and he prefaced it with the words: "The kingdom of heaven is like this." What could he possibly mean? With what kind of ears do we hear this parable today?

A little later in the same chapter Matthew offers us an explanation. The details of the little story are spelled out, and the story is allegorized in simple terms. "The man who sowed the good seed is the Son of Man; the field is the world; the good seed is the people who belong to the Kingdom; the weeds are the people who belong to the Evil One; and the enemy who sowed the weeds is the Devil" so it goes on to the end of the story. It sounds to me much more like an explanation given by a zealous interpreter of the early Church than a comment of Jesus. Somehow it seems out of style for him; and his parables are very rarely allegories like this. But even if we accept this as an interpretation given by Jesus, we are still left with a lot of questions unanswered. And we still need to hear what this vivid story is telling us about life under the rule of God in our world today.

As I read it again and again I found it speaking to me about the one central baffling question that has been asked since human beings began to think. It is a question that the greatest minds of every generation keep wrestling with, a question that has stimulated the most sublime works of art in every civilization—dramas, novels, music, painting, sculpture—and a question that every one of us has asked from the moment we began to reflect on the world into which we have been born. In simple terms it is: "Who put the weeds in God's garden?" If you prefer to call it: "The problem of theodicy and the etiology of evil" that's all right too. But, I'll stick with "Who put the weeds in God's garden?" coupled with the naturally ensuing question: "What can be done about it?" Those are the two questions raised for me by this tale of Jesus'.

The Bible, as you know, opens with a magnificent picture of divine creation and then offers us the Garden of Eden as a symbol of human life under the rule of God. In a paradise where everything grows in harmony with God's design and perfectly reflects his purpose in creation, man and woman appear as the unique creatures to whom is given the privilege of communion with the Creator in whose image they are made. To them is committed the care of the Garden under the rule of God. They are his stewards, and in obedience to him (an obedience that is tested by one simple taboo) they are to explore and enjoy the mysteries and glories of the garden. They are also to enjoy one another spiritually, mentally and physically, and found a human family under the loving rule of God.

This is the Paradise, the Garden of Eden, the Golden Age, the vision of life without violence, without suffering, without selfishness, ugliness, and fear, that dances like a mirage before each succeeding generation. We are all born with a nostalgia for the Garden, and every religion has its tale of how it may be found. For Christians and Jews it is a Kingdom which was and is to come but for both the great question is: where is it now?

For the weeds have come. The poison has contaminated the Garden. The snake, the shadowy stranger, came, and then there was sin. A century ago in our western civilization, it became popular to stand this story on its head. There was no original Garden of Innocence, but a primitive bestiality, and the march of history is one of gradual elimination of the poisonous weeds on the way to the utopia ahead.

In Tennyson's words we are to "move upwards working out the beast, and let the ape and tiger die." So we are gradually to arrive at the "far-off divine event to which the whole creation moves." At that time there were strong hopes that the advance of human knowledge would slowly but inevitably weed out the evils from which humanity suffers—disease, hunger, crime, and war. These weeds in the garden came from ignorance and the lingering traces of our animal heritage. A generation ago the historian-philosopher H.G. Wells could still write his 'Outline of History' in this optimistic mood.

How remote this all seems from the mood of today. It would be hard to find any thoughtful person with such a happy faith in the moral evolution of humankind. Wells himself, after the shock of Buchenwald and Hiroshima, entitled his last book 'Mankind at the End of the Tether', and it was a manifesto of utter hopelessness, a capitulation to the weeds. Christians should find no pleasure in saying to the disillusioned believers in the humanist paradise "I told you so." For too often the churches had adjusted their theology to fit this belief in moral progress and had interpreted Jesus' teaching about the Kingdom of God to accord with the secularist utopia. What then, do we say today in answer to the question "Where do the weeds come from?"

"It was some enemy who did this." Despite all my theological education to the contrary I cannot keep from coming back to the belief that there is something in the Biblical idea of the personification of evil, a real Devil. My experience during over five decades in the ministry has not changed my mind. The shadowy stranger who invades the garden is a reality—as he certainly was to Jesus.

I know the risks involved in giving this simple answer to the question: "Who put the weeds in God's Garden?" If you say "The Devil" you offer yourself a beautiful excuse for your sins. "And the Lord said unto the woman, 'What is this that you have done?' And the woman said, 'The serpent beguiled me, and I did eat.'" I would simply note that the Lord did not accept the excuse, and we know very well that it is a sham. More worrying is the tendency among the hyper-orthodox to say: "The Devil is in power in this world, causing all the horrors we read about, so there's nothing we can do about them." There are some very strong voices to be heard in this country today opposing all attempts to eliminate war and promote justice on the grounds that these things must be until the Judgement and the return of Christ. "No weeding," they say, on the basis of this parable, "Christ will do that when he comes."

If I thought that a belief in the Devil would inevitably lead to such moral abdication and paralysis in the face of immediate evils, I would shut up on the subject. But I don't. Neither did Jesus who understood the power of the Devil as no one else, yet he fought every evil in sight. Neither did those great evangelicals two centuries ago who combined an understanding of the Devil with a determination to alleviate the miseries of the poor and to liberate the slaves. Of course, there have been cruelties and absurdities connected with belief in a personal devil—as there have been connected with our belief in Almighty God. Witch hunting, necromancy, orgies of so called exorcism—all these things haunt us and make many thoughtful Christians suspicious of the current revival of demonology and the occult. Yet, I am convinced that behind the words, "It was some enemy that did this," lies a truth that is deeper and more adequate to our present situation, than any other answer presently being offered to the age old mystery of iniquity. I hope, however, that none of you shares the feeling of an old Scottish lady who remarked about her minister: "It is such a comfort to have a preacher who believes in a personal devil."

Some time ago I came across a book entitled: "The Devil: Perceptions of Evil from Antiquity to Primitive Christianity." I began reading it assuming that it would be a scholarly inquiry into an old superstition. It is by Jeffrey Russell, who was Professor of Medieval Studies at the University of Notre Dame. It was indeed scholarly, but I was surprised to read these words which seem to me of enormous importance for our Christian understanding today. "The Devil is no quaint or outmoded figure, but a phenomenon of enormous and perennial power in, or over, the human spirit. It may be that the growth of interest and belief in the Devil today marks a growing perception of the reality that is evil. By understanding the principle behind this evil, by coming to know the Devil better, we will be able to understand—and combat—the evil that confronts each of us as individuals."

To that I say 'amen'. Before I read it I was hearing just this message as I listened to the parable of the weeds. I am not at all interested in any attempt to describe the Devil, nor do I insist that you must use this name to describe the fearful and malign power that has invaded the garden of God and scattered his poisonous seeds. It's just that I believe it is good for us to know what we are up against. I have come to believe that we confront a quality and intensity of evil that cannot be fully accounted for by human folly and selfishness. Life under the rule of God cannot, while we are here on earth, be abstracted from this Kingdom of Evil that surrounds us. The Church, representing the Kingdom of God, cannot be a pure and uncontaminated society. Every attempt through the years to create a perfect Garden of God has been doomed to failure. "You can't get rid of all the weeds just like that" says our parable; "only the final judgement will do the purging." I hear again the voice of Jesus warning us against doing our own judging and sorting out. That belongs to the Lord alone and comes in his good time. What we have to do now is to be alert to the powers of evil, and to equip ourselves to resist the Devil where we can. "Be vigilant," we read in the First Epistle of Peter, "because your adversary the Devil, as a roaring lion, walketh about, seeking whom he may devour."

How then do we deal with him? The Bible offers us the surprising answer. We are to treat him as a defeated foe. The Old Testament, with all its emphasis on the hideous ravages of evil, keeps sounding the note of the final victory of God's Kingdom. "Say to them that are of a fearful heart: 'Be Strong, and fear not; behold your God will come with vengeance...he will come and save you...And the ransomed of the Lord shall return, and come to Zion with songs and everlasting joy upon their heads: they shall obtain joy and gladness; and sorrow and sighing shall flee away.'" This is the ultimate fulfillment of a life under God, the triumph of his Kingdom. And in the last book of the Bible there comes ringing through the weird tangle of symbols and cryptic sayings the triumph song of the Kingdom of God and the dying gasp of a Devil defeated and destroyed.

This comes to us as something more than a pious hope. For it is anchored in the decisive campaign that was waged by Jesus two thousand years ago. He began, you remember, with a decisive encounter with a Devil who was for him very real and very threatening and never left him alone until that final moment in Gethsemane when the Lord used the words that are the key to the Kingdom: "Not my will but thine be done." Then he moved to his decisive confrontation with the powers of evil. For three hours on Calvary the Devil had his way, and his appalling powers over our hearts and minds were exposed as never before or since. But for Jesus this was the darkest moment before the dawn, the grim defeat that was to be turned into final victory. Do you remember the words he spoke as he went to the cross? "Now is the judgement of this world: now shall the prince of this world be cast out." (John 12:31 KJ)

We are surely called to deal with the Devil as a power whose nerve has been cut, and of whom we need not be afraid. The authentic attitude of the Christian facing the rampant evils and dire threats that surround us is that of Martin Luther over four and a half centuries ago:

> *"And though this world, with devils filled,*
> *Should threaten to undo us,*
> *We will not fear, for God hath willed*
> *his truth to triumph through us.*
> *The prince of darkness grim,*
> *we tremble not for him:*
> *His rage we can endure;*
> *for lo his doom is sure.*
> *One little word shall fell him."*
> *That little word is JESUS!*

Chapter 17

Life After Death

Philip of Macedon had a slave to whom he gave a standing order. The slave was to come into the king's chamber every morning, no matter what the king was doing, and say to him in a loud voice: "Philip, remember that thou must die." Few of us need such a melancholy reminder, for we all know that we shall live relatively few years on this earth and then die. But all of us have questions about death, and both our minds and hearts crave satisfying answers.

This mysterious, often frightening fact raises some of life's most urgent questions. What is the meaning of death to us and to God? What lies beyond, if anything? Will we recognize our loved ones? Is death merely a solemn, dark curtain rung down on the stage of this all too brief earthly life? Or is it the lifting of the curtain on the most wonderful act of life's drama? If God really cares for us, why has no one returned to tell us the truth about life after death?

Whether Paul found answers for his mind's questions before or after his heart found its unswerving faith we do not know. But this we know: his faith made him victorious over the fear of death. In writing to the Romans, he spoke in these unforgettable words of his unconquerable faith: "For I am sure that neither death...nor anything else in all creation will be able to separate us from the love of God in Jesus Christ our Lord."

If we would make this faith our own, we must first of all begin by accepting death as a fact, albeit a mysterious one. Far too many philosophers and teachers of religion have tried to show that death is not quite real. Christianity does not teach us that death is unreal, or that it brings no pain;

but that its pain, loss and heartbreak can be overcome by faith in Christ. We are not to pretend that death brings no rending of the heart, but we are expected as Christians to say with Paul: "For I am sure that neither death...nor anything else in all creation will be able to separate us from the love of God in Christ Jesus our Lord."

Of all the experiences of humankind death is the most certain. It may come soon or in lingering weakness, but come death will; and it knocks at the door of pauper and millionaire alike. The bell tolls sometime for every one of us.

The mystification regarding the Great Adventure troubles many hearts. They cry out for some satisfying certainty regarding their loved ones who have gone on before. Human nature almost breaks under the weight of sorrow's burden and love's tragedy.

Since death is so common and so inevitable it is strange that our thoughts and attitudes regarding it are still largely unchristian. The great majority of people look upon death as an unutterable woe and a baffling enemy.

Is death an unrelieved tragedy? I cannot think so. Death lends grandeur and fruitfulness to life. Affection deepens because it lives in the shadow of an impending separation. Friends and families love with a deeper love because the sun shines on them but for a reason; men and women work with a higher intensity and grander seriousness because time marches on relentlessly toward the end of the earthly drama.

If we were undiscriminatingly immortal, we would be tempted to live in gladsome idleness in a world that had neither gravity nor greatness. With the idea of death, new meaning steals into life. How else can we be made to realize the immensity, the earnestness, the essential dignity of living?

Mortality is a constituent part of human nature. Our bodies have time limits set in them by the gracious and wise hand of the Creator, and death is no more unnatural than birth. If we could see it as our Father sees it, we should not count it as a human penalty, but a divine release. No! physical death is one of the mercies of our blessed Creator.

We should not fear the loss of these frail habitations of the flesh, for God has promised to give us a body "even as it pleased him."

The butterfly, released by a process of nature from its binding, blinding prison house, flies in the vastness of a new world of freedom and light, reflecting on iridescent wings the golden sunlight of a new universe of unimagined beauty; nor does it sigh again for the old outworn cocoon which it leaves behind on the threshold of its new adventure. So shall it be with the soul when God shall open the door and set us free, and we shall come into the full glory of the resurrection body.

Where are our loved ones who have fallen asleep in Christ? Many an anxious heart cries out for an answer. They have simply gone out of the body into the spirit. They have dropped the impediments of the flesh to dwell in the freedom of spiritual existence. They are not wandering aimlessly upon some distant celestial shore. They are in God; they are in the fellowship of Christ; they are living in a spiritual body perfectly adapted for their glorified and redeemed life. If they are with God, they are with us, for God is not far off, but closer than breathing and nearer than hands and feet. They surround us as a great cloud of witnesses, beholding us from within the veil, ministering to our innermost hearts, a part of the great spiritual universe which presses upon us and beckons us ever onward and upward. They are the guests of God and they await our homecoming when we too shall enter into the gates of life.

Surely Dr. Fosdick is correct when he declares: "Death is not a period that brings the sentence of life to a full stop; it is only a comma that punctuates life to a loftier significance."

In the Gospel of John it is recorded that Jesus said: "I am the resurrection and the life: He that believeth in me, though he were dead, yet shall he live. And whosoever liveth and believeth in me shall never die. Believest thou this?" (John 11:25,26 KJ) Do you believe it? I do!

I once knew a family who had inherited a grand piano. There it sat in the living room, carefully waxed and regularly tuned, but no one in the house knew how to play it; except one member of the family, who if called upon, could thump out a passable version of "My Country, 'Tis of Thee." There sat that magnificent instrument which could have filled the house with glorious music. But all that was ever heard from it was one little tune, rather hesitatingly rendered.

That's a parable of our situation. The Resurrection Faith is capable of filling our lives all of the time with glorious music. Instead, all the use we make of it is to play one little tune once in awhile. The great truth is that the Lord Jesus Christ could not be holden of death; God did raise him up; his victory over death is the promise of eternal life that lasts forever!

We are talking here about something that is very personal and applies to each of us on an individual basis. That is the reason we say in the Apostles' Creed: "I believe in the resurrection of the body." If it were not so, if we did not have this kind of faith, then we would be subject to all the illusions and temptations that characterize such eccentricities as spiritualism, with its squeaking ghosts and shivering tables, and all that type of thing. But in the Christian religion we are talking about persons. We believe that the resurrection of Jesus Christ was the resurrection of a real person to a real personal life on a higher and more wonderful level. And so it shall be with all those who are committed to Christ.

When we say, "I believe in the resurrection of the body," we are saying that life that is cut off (as it seems to us), has its great opportunity yet before it. This life shall still truly flower and bloom. God who loves in a deeper way than we know how to love, gathers up this life and gives it the heavenly body which is the vehicle for the expression of personality, so that this person can live and find a greater fulfillment. This is our Christian faith.

One of our great and searching problems is the problem of bereavement. We may be able to stand sturdily and bravely up to life with regard to ourselves, with regard to our own disappointments, but, when we see loved ones taken from us, what then? We want to know if they are lost to us forever, or will we see them again? When we say, "I believe in the resurrection of the body," the answer is 'yes.' When loved ones are lost, there is the chance to see the loved one again if we have faith in the God in whose hands we are.

"In what manner of body?" someone asks. And here is the Apostle Paul's answer: "God gives a body as it pleases him." Whenever I read that verse, I relax. Some things we can safely leave to God. We do not have to answer all the minute questions of how this universe is run. Some things you can trust God to know; some things you can trust God to do.

The New Testament is certain that the relation of the body to the life hereafter is like that of the chrysalis to the butterfly, or the egg to the chick, or the bulb to the gorgeous lily. St. Paul emphatically declares: "…we know that if the earthly tent we live in is destroyed, we have a building of God, a house not made with hands, eternal in the heavens." It is the Christian faith, that when the soul moves from this earthly house of the physical body. it takes up it abode in a spiritual dwelling that is as superior to the body as the chick is to the egg; or the fragrant, inspiring lily is to the ugly, dead-like bulb; or the iridescent butterfly on soaring wings is to the awkward, earthbound, static chrysalis. It is the Christian certainty that personality goes on despite bodily changes, including the bodily change we call death.

If we need a body to express personality in this life so that we can see each other, and speak through it and listen through it, and if we need the equivalent of an earthly body in order that we may know social fellowship and growth and understanding in heaven, certainly God knows how to take care of it. God gives you a body as you need it. Life goes on and your personality goes on and that is the thing that really matters. If we can think of God's eternal life as a place where there is personal identity and where there is recognition, then we have what we need in this great phrase, "the resurrection of the body."

One time I heard the story of a little boy in New Haven, Connecticut who was saying his prayers. He prayed: "our Father who art in New Haven, how did you know my name…"

His words were mixed up, but in a very real sense, he was expressing what our Christian faith does say to us. God is present with us, wherever we are; and He knows each of us personally, by name. This is basic to our faith. God knows and cares what happens to us.

Benjamin Franklin put this truth most cogently in an Epitaph which he once wrote for himself. In it he declared: "The body of B. Franklin, like the cover of an old book, its contents torn out and stripped of its letters and gilding, lies here. But his work shall not be wholly lost; for it will, as he believed, appear once more in a new and more perfect edition, corrected and amended by God the Author." Surely God did not make us to abandon us!

The Christian faith declares with confidence that this world is "a home for the rearing of persons, not…a gallow on which ultimately they will all be hanged." It insists that life and not death has the final word. That, in the nutshell of one sentence, is our message of hope—"life and not death has the final word."

Life After Death

"O Love that wilt not let me go,
I rest my weary soul in thee;
I give Thee back the life I owe,
That in thine ocean depths its flow
May richer, fuller be.

O Light that followest all my way,
I yield my flickering torch to Thee;
My heart restores its borrowed ray,
That in Thy sunshine's blaze its day
May brighter, fairer be.

O joy that seekest me through pain,
I cannot close my heart to thee;
I trace the rainbow through the rain,
And feel the promise is not vain
That morn shall tearless be.

O Cross that liftest up my head,
I dare not ask to fly from thee;
I lay in dust life's glory dead,
And from the ground there blossoms red
Life that shall endless be."

This I Believe

Chapter 18
I Thought You'd Never Ask

Whenever I get into a discussion of religion and what I believe, inevitably there are questions people ask about Creation, Heaven and Hell, the Second Coming, the Rapture, Miracles, Extra Terrestrial Life, Cyberspace, and a host of others. Without going into great length about any one of these I would like to tell you what I believe about some of them.

<u>How did it all begin</u>? Must we choose between the ages of rock, and the Rock of Ages?

The scientists tell us how the world was made and approximately how long it took to make the earth and to form living things (including humans). The Bible tells us who (that is, God) designed the processes by which all came into being, and it also tells us for what purpose he made them. The Bible tells us that God made the heavens and the earth, but it does not tell us how it was made.

The following list suggests the continuing creative acts of God in the history of our earth and living things.
- Five billion years ago God created the earth and the moon.
- Four billion years ago God created the sea.
- Three billion two hundred million years ago God willed into being the DNA molecule—stands for deoxyribose nucleic acid—the secret of life; and algae and bacteria appear in the water.
- Six hundred million years ago fish and invertebrate animals appear.
- Two hundred million years ago birds are created.
- Forty million years ago monkeys and apes evolve.
- Two to three million years ago—Homo erectus, the first man ("Adam" of Genesis 1) via God's use of DNA in ever more complex forms appears.

- One hundred thousand years ago Cro-Magnon man in Europe, North and South America populated by Asian hunters.
- Nine thousand B.C. Jericho settled.
- Seven thousand three hundred B.C. man learns to cultivate wheat and barley in the Near East.
- Six thousand B.C. cattle are domesticated.
- Three thousand five hundred B.C. Bronze Age.
- Two thousand six hundred B.C. Pyramids of Egypt are built.
- Two thousand four hundred B.C. Stonehenge.
- Two thousand B.C. Eskimo Culture.
- One thousand four hundred B.C. Iron Age in the Near East.
- One thousand two hundred and fifty B.C. Moses introduces Monotheism and the Ten Commandments.

Human beings were created after God's magnificently designed DNA molecule had produced thousands of forms of life; God's brilliant creation of the DNA brought all kinds of flora and fauna to his universe and our earth. Humankind was a high point of God's creative action.

In and through Jesus Christ God has revealed the goal of his creation of humankind. God's will and purpose in creation was the development of persons who would respond in faith and love to his presence and will; to the extent that they, through the influence and saving power of Jesus, would be Christ-like persons.

<u>Heaven and Hell and The Ascension</u>: Modern man believes our universe is probably finite, bounded, and elliptical in shape. The Universe is composed of millions of solar systems. This is quite a different view of the world than that conceived by the biblical writers.

At one time ancients believed in three, sometimes seven, different heavens. The earth was flat and God was transcendent, far removed from the concerns of earth.

I Thought You'd Never Ask

Titove, the first Russian spaceman to go around the earth in a spacecraft declared: "I have searched the heavens but could find no angels, nor could I find the throne of God." Of course he couldn't. The throne of God isn't up in the sky, nor is God "up there" somewhere in the sky. God is spirit. God is non-physical. God is not localized. God is all around us. We need to affirm the affirmation of Christmas—"Immanuel—God with us."

Talking once about the picture of Jesus a person said Jesus should be shown with white hair, because Revelation 1:14 states that his hair is white as snow. But consider the rest of the verse: "...his eyes were like a flame of fire, his feet like burnished bronze...from his mouth issued a sharp two edged sword." This is obviously a metaphor rather than an actual portrayal.

Hawthorne tells the story of Rappaccini's daughter. A botanist fed his daughter poison so she would be invulnerable and able to help him with experiments. Eventually she noted that she could kill insects just by breathing on them. Then she fell in love, but she dared not approach her loved one or kiss him. I think of this story whenever I read the account in Revelation that Christ will slay his enemies with the breath of his lips. We must not take this literally, or we will lose forever the beauty of the life giving breath of God envisioned by Ezekiel when he wrote: "Breathe on me breath of God, fill me with life anew."

How does one get close to God? Does a person get close to God by climbing Mt. Everest, 29,3000 feet above sea level? Or by flying in a plane more than 30,000 feet above sea level? I have flown like that and there were people aboard filled with spirits, but not the spirit of God.

I recall the story of one of our astronauts who told of taking communion as his space craft circles the moon for the first time. His pastor had made prior arrangements so that this astronaut with his family and pastor—some 240,000 miles away—would commune together at the same time with the Risen Lord: and Christ, the Risen Lord, was at both places at the same time.

Yes, God is on his throne, or more correctly his thrones, for he is enthroned in the hearts of people. To enthrone God in our hearts is to make him and his purposes the authority for our decision making in all matters.

Affirming our modern view of the heavens and the earth, what happened that day when Jesus ascended from the midst of his disciples? Did he ascend to a third or seventh heaven and sit on the right hand of God?

In I Corinthians 15 I believe Paul makes it clear that Jesus was a spirit (glorified) body after the resurrection. He was no longer subject to the categories of time and space. He was not hampered by locked doors. Wherever men would receive him, the dear Lord enters in.

We have given up the notion of a physical heaven far up in the sky; but we still hold to the kingdom of heaven which includes those persons of faith who have died before us as well as those who are living now—persons who have made their choice to be in Christ's kingdom.

It is during our lives that we make the choice as to whose kingdom we will identify our lives, our money, our time, our talents, our prayers. The time of decision making is the time of entering the Kingdom of Heaven. The Kingdom of Heaven is within you, said Jesus.

So, Heaven is a spirit realm where persons who have chosen Christ as their Savior and Lord continue to live in his presence, both in this world and in the life everlasting. We need to decide who governs our earth and our universe. It is my firm conviction that we and our earth are under the reign of God and his Christ, the Risen Lord, yesterday, today, and forevermore. I believe: "This Is My Father's World." This is quite different from the view of those who would interpret the Apocalyptic writings in the

I Thought You'd Never Ask

Bible as saying Jesus has turned over the world to the Devil for a time. I do not believe Jesus has to wait a millennium or two to reign. The Lord Jesus reigns now.

We must be very careful in reading and understanding such Apocalyptic writings as Daniel and the Book of Revelation. Apocalypse means hidden—hence it suggests mystery; and the vivid pictorial language used by these writers has lent itself to a great deal of abuse—particularly by some of our popular radio and TV evangelists. The most popular of these wide eyed Evangelists who are hoodwinking millions of gullible listeners and viewers every week, approach the Book of Revelation from the point of view that if you have the key to unlock the mysteries of the secret code you can decipher the future and identify the date of the end of the world. And of course, they believe they have that key.

This point of view must be repudiated entirely. It is blasphemous, presumptuous, and unscriptural. It flies in the very face of Scripture itself. Paul, quoting the words of Jesus, insists that the time of the end is unknown to us all. Those who with their pious charts and their pontificating predictions treat the Book of Revelation like a celestial slide rule revealing the date and the hour of the end of time are blasphemous. They claim more knowledge than Jesus himself. There is no legitimacy, no Bible base, for this line of interpretation. The Book of Revelation is not a timetable to be read like an airline schedule, telling us when we can expect the final end to arrive.

Sometimes when asked about Heaven and Hell I have likened it to a man and wife whose relationship has gone askew. In such a case we often refer to one or the other "being in the dog house." This estrangement is like hell. It means being apart from the one you love. It seems as though your world has dropped out from under you. So it is with those who for whatever reason are estranged from

This I Believe

God. They are separated from the one who truly loves them. They are estranged; they are spiritually in the "dog house." As long as they continue to deny God's love; as long as they insist on their own way; as long as they continue to feel that they do not need God; just so long they will continue to dwell in that far off land while the Father waits anxiously hoping to be able to welcome his child home again.

But what about "<u>The Rapture</u>?" Some writers on Revelation and some radio and TV preachers state that the "Rapture" will soon take place. The Rapture refers to those Christians who have died in Christ who will be resurrected and join living Christians, all of whom will be caught up together in the clouds with Jesus. (Thessalonians 4:15-18)

Imagine the fear this creates in the minds of children who face the possibility that their parents may be snatched up into heaven leaving them behind.

One writer set the date for the Rapture by taking as his key date May 15, 1948, when Israel became a nation and about ten percent or less of the Jews returned to Israel. He then added one generation (forty years), and came up with 1988 as the date scheduled for the Rapture. Others have used different formulae, and all have been equally disappointed.

But what does all that do to our belief in Parousia or the presence of the Risen Lord? If Christ, the Risen Lord, is with us now, what gain is there in being drawn up into the sky to be with him?

John in Revelation having written about things that were and things that are, finally portrays the things that are to be. This is where we must ponder the meaning of the Second Coming. Have you considered what the Risen Lord, who is with us now, would do if he physically came into our midst? What would he start trying to do that he is not trying to do right now? Is God working out his triumph and victory now, or must we wait for the 'hereafter' or the Second Coming? Isn't he trying to win our hearts, our motives, attitudes now?

We affirm the basic message of the apocalypse, namely: a steady faith in the unfailing purposes of God, and in his final victory over unrighteousness. God's love in us is the only enduring force in our universe. The future belongs to God and his Risen Christ.

We pray—Come Lord Jesus; and he does come. We are caught up, not in the sky, but in his purposes, hopes, yearnings, and yes, his prayers for our world. We become friends and co-workers with him here on earth, and we declare once more Immanuel—God with us!

The struggle between good and evil will go on as long as there is life as we know it on earth. We cannot know when it will end for no one knows the day nor the hour, but we do know that all "things" are perishable. When time shall be no more, and heaven and earth shall pass away then will come the final triumph of Righteousness. God alone will be the victor, and those who dwell with him in his kingdom on earth and in heaven will share in the glory and triumph of that day.

<u>Miracles</u>: Of course I believe in miracles. We witness them every day, particularly when we see what modern medicine is able to accomplish. On the other hand, if you ask me if I believe that God intervenes to miraculously save one life and leave another to die I would have to confess to some doubts. For example, there is an automobile accident in which two teenagers are involved—one is killed and the other spared. How often in similar circumstances I have heard a parent declare: "I thank God for sparing my child." What about the parent of the other child? Are you going to say that God deliberately performed a miracle—choosing to spare the one and not the other? I cannot believe that a God of love would so choose between two of his children.

One life is spared and the other dies because of the circumstances of the accident.

Lightning strikes one house and destroys it while the neighbor's home is unharmed. This sort of happening is not because of God's choosing, but because that is the kind of world we live in. To believe that God is in his heaven manipulating all of life's happenings would be to make of us human beings created in God's likeness mere puppets, and would deprive life of its meaning and purpose.

Miracles? Yes, God working through science and human spirits can do things we often think are impossible!

<u>Extra-terrestrial Life</u>: Since 1961 when the first manned orbital flight into space was made there has been a great deal of speculation as to whether or not there is life on any other planet, and if so, what does that do to our belief about God. The scientific assumption is that life is not unique to earth. The whole universe is full of God's creative acts. The raw material which God uses for the development of life (DNA) is in abundance throughout the universe. This is the universal language of life, and we believe that all things were created by God.

If God created intelligent life on other planets Genesis one might be expanded to read: "God created not only mankind, but also intelligent beings in his universe. Beings with spirituality."

If this is so the probability is that intelligent life on various planets exists on different levels of achievement. We need to ask what is the nature of intelligent beings created in the image of God?

To be created in the image of God means that a creature shares some of the spiritual potentialities which are in the divine spirit, God. If there is life on other planets we now ask if some of those living creatures are intelligent. Can they distinguish between what is true and false? Are they able to choose between what is ethically right or wrong? Do they experience moral choice? Do they have eyes and possibly color cones so they can experience beautifully colored objects? Can they differentiate between what is ugly and what is beautiful? Can they relate to their creator? Do they experience a relationship which gives them a sense of awe and wonder as expressed by an Einstein or a Psalmist? Do they exhibit human qualities? Do they share a sense of loyalty, honor, justice, mercy, kindness, selflessness or cooperativeness? How intelligent are they?

You cannot develop mathematics to a high degree without the ability to think abstractly and of concrete needs and applications. So language (the ability to read, write and communicate) would be an inevitable corollary of their intelligence.

My God is super galactic. There is only one God of the universe. He is the creator of the 250 billion stars in our galaxy, and the creator of billions of galaxies. This is my Father's Universe and I can hear him "speak" everywhere, "O Lord, my God, How Great Thou Art!"

Paul in writing to the Colossians (1:15-20) was stating that Christ is Christ of the whole universe. A loving God who created all things, and we must assume that if he created intelligent beings on other planets they are also in his image. Then they must have the capacity for truth, goodness, beauty and faith. Let us teach our children to trust all God's creatures who are endowed with abilities for intelligence, aesthetics, truth and faith, especially those who are engaged in the disciplines of life fulfillment.

And what about cyberspace? Are we going to see the end of worshipping congregations as we now know them to be replaced by "cyberchurches?" As a Time Magazine (12/16/96) article queries: "Is it possible that God in a network age will look, somehow, different?" According to this article some believe the "Internet" is a world of its own, a new metaphor for God, crafted by humans but growing out of control. (A Frankenstein's monster? one might ask.) One professor quoted says: "If you believe in an eternal, unchanging God, you'll be in trouble."

In reaction, I believe that just as in the matter of extraterrestrial life we have to keep our minds open to where these developments in Communication will lead us. Nevertheless I cannot accept any notion that makes God the creation of the human mind, rather than the other way around. God in his wonder has created humans with minds of incalculable possibilities to continue the mighty acts of his creation, but God is still in control. I believe this is my Father's world or universe if you will, and that includes "cyberspace." The challenge we face is to learn how to use his creation to further his Kingdom of Righteousness, Love, and Brotherhood.

As far as a "cyberchurch" replacing our "places" of worship I believe that Christianity is a religion of persons and that we need fellowship with other persons. I believe that this is best found when two or three are physically gathered together, and that the "unreal" world of cyberspace will never be able to replace the coming together of "the faithful" to worship Almighty God in the beauty of holiness as they break bread together and drink of the Cup as they remember the Lord Jesus Christ.

Chapter 19

He Is Risen

One time I saw a copy of a most amazing newspaper. It was called, "The Jerusalem Daily News." The date on it was a Sunday in the year A.D. 33. A startling headline covered the top of the front page: "Nazarene's Tomb Found Empty." Secondary headlines read: "Earthquake rends city as Prophet Dies"; "Crucified King of the Jews seen Alive Is Report." A front page editorial said: "Last Friday the city of Jerusalem witnessed what we believe will go down in history as the world's most atrocious crime. Today a mysterious sequel to the story—The Prophet's Tomb found empty. What does this empty tomb mean?" So read a part of the front page of "The Jerusalem Daily News."

Listen! Can't you hear the newsboys of Jerusalem on the streets that morning, crying out: "Read all about it, 'Tombs Empty', 'Crucified One Seen Alive,' 'Death Vanquished, say the converts.'"

Of course, it will not surprise you to learn that this startling newspaper was printed recently. It was a modern man's attempt to bring the Easter story to life. It was an obvious effort to arrest the attention of people today, to catch their minds and their imaginations so that they would hear and believe the Easter story of the Risen Christ.

Even the modern radio has joined the attempt to break through our Easter doubts and skepticism. On the Saturday night before Easter several years ago, I was startled to hear the newscaster at eleven o'clock say: "And now, ladies and gentlemen, here is the greatest news story of all history: 'The stone was found rolled away from the tomb!'"

Every preacher in his or her pulpit on Easter morning likewise has the wish for some means, some device by

This I Believe

which to arrest the attention of the congregation, to catch their hearts and minds with the truth of Easter, that then and there and forever after they will know the redeeming joy of Christian Faith. The minister in the pulpit on Easter feels as the wartime chaplain did who had a boy pause before him, just before the young man went over the top and onto the battlefield, and say to him: "Quick Padre, tell me something about God." At Easter we want to say something that will touch many lives and make them better, happier, deeper, richer, stronger, that will bring to them the life changing faith of the Living Christ.

Are there such words that can do this, that can perform this miracle, so to speak? Yes, I believe there are. They are not new words, but very old ones. They are contained, not in a modern book, but in the New Testament story. In a way, the New Testament was the newspaper of Jerusalem. It was not called the "Daily News," but the "Good News," the Gospel. That's what Gospel means: "Good News." The disciples went about with this story, saying: "Let us give you the Gospel, the Good News." It was the best news ever heard. It is still the Good News—dramatic, arresting, life changing, personal. But to hear it, to truly hear it, we need to take the grave clothes off our minds and imaginations. We will have to get out of the deadly tomb of suspicion and fear, and listen with faith and expectancy to the greatest News Story of All History.

It tells of how, after Christ was crucified on Calvary Hill, and buried in the tomb, he arose from his grave and appeared many times to his disciples as the Risen Christ.

How he appeared, I do not know. How he looked, I am not sure. Yet his followers who knew him best recognized him. They were sure. Before his appearance, they were skeptical, beaten people. After they met the Risen Christ, they became new people, the bravest band that ever marched the earth.

He Is Risen

After the Resurrection, he appeared first of all to Mary Magdalene at the tomb. She stood without the sepulchre weeping that first Easter morn. And she saw Jesus, who said: "Woman, why are you weeping?" She, supposing him to be the gardener, replied: "Sir, if you have carried him away, tell me where you have laid him, and I will take him away." And Jesus said: "Mary." Then she recognized his voice, and said: "Rabboni," which means master.

In this exact same way, the Living Christ meets us today amidst our sorrows. Death is still our greatest fear; the source of our deepest anxieties.

"Thou madest man, he knows not why.
He thinks he was not made to die."

Facing the death of dear ones, of our friends, or our own death, we often look to the sepulchre without hope. At that instant, the Risen Christ speaks to us as he spoke to Mary, if we will listen, "Because I live, you shall live also."

Our hope of immortality is in him. In his life and death and resurrection, we have the living assurance that there is more of life than this present world. Through faith in him, we have "life and immortality brought to light through the Gospel." He does not make us immortal, but he awakens us to the immortal destiny which God has put in each of us. If we will but hear with faith, like Mary we will recognize his voice saying to us: "In my Father's house are many mansions; if it were not so, I would have told you. I go to prepare a place for you." The joy and hope of immortality is in his living presence.

That Easter afternoon, the New Testament relates, he appeared to the two disciples walking down to Emmaus. The disciples were discouraged and downcast. As they walked, Jesus overtook them and asked why they were so sad as they talked. They did not recognize him and so they related the story of the crucifixion and the rumor of the resurrection which they couldn't believe. Then Christ began interpreting the Scripture to them and finally stopped at their house. As they broke bread together, their eyes were opened and they knew him. Then he vanished out of their sight, and they said to one another: "Did not our hearts burn within us as he walked with us and while he opened the Scriptures to us?" So he transformed the hearts of the discouraged disciples.

So also, in this present age, the Living Christ comes to walk with us amidst our discouragements. There is not one of us who does not, now and again, fight the struggle of discouragement and depressed spirits. Discouragement is one of humankind's greatest enemies. This is borne out in an old legend that relates how Satan was once selling off his tools. Finally, he came to his last and meanest looking tool. It was the tool of discouragement with which he pried into people's lives. The story says the price was so high that no one bought it and so Satan still uses discouragement as his most potent tool.

And discouragement's most potent enemy is the Living Christ. In the grandeur of his courage, we will find new courage. In the power that turns thorns to crowns, we find new power. In the strength of God that overcomes even a Cross, we are made, through Christ, able to overcome our crosses. So Father Tyrell once said: "Often I am tempted to give up the struggle of life, but the sight of that strange Man on his cross sends me back again and again."

In his living presence, we too, walk our Emmaus Road of discouragement and, by his love, our hearts burn with new courage and faith.

He appeared also to Simon Peter at the seaside. After the crucifixion, Peter went back to his old trade as a fisherman. His hope of the Kingdom had been destroyed; his dearest friend executed.

He Is Risen

While he and his friends toiled at the nets, someone, perhaps a merchant, called out from shore: "Friends, have you caught any fish?" "No," they answered. Then he said: "Cast your nets on the other side of the boat." They did and ran into a school of fish. Peter looked back to shore. Sure enough, it was the Lord. With all of his old impulsiveness, he leaped from the boat and swam to shore to see him.

The living Christ had appeared to Peter and his companions in the midst of their daily work. The living Christ walks with us today in our daily work. Often we, like Peter, fail to recognize him. Yet he walks with us as surely in the Market Place as in the House of Prayer. He is our companion as much in daily toil as in Sunday worship. The Christian Faith is not departmentalized. We live that faith out in our daily work. We express our love of God in daily serving our fellow beings in the Spirit of Christ.

That same morning, Christ said to Simon Peter: "Lovest thou me?" and Simon answered: "Yes, Lord, thou knowest." Then Jesus replied: "Feed my lambs, feed my sheep." So our daily tasks become a trust from God: to serve Christ is to serve others in his name and spirit. Still he says today as he walks with us in our daily work: "Lovest thou me? Feed my sheep."

He appeared unto Thomas, the doubter. Thomas had heard that the Risen Lord had appeared after the Resurrection, but he would not believe it. He said: "Until I see the side, I will not believe." Eight days later, Christ appeared unto the disciples, and Thomas was present. He said to Thomas: "Reach hither your finger and thrust your hand in my side. Be not faithless, but believing." Thomas said: "My Lord and my God." Christ said: "Because you have seen, you have believed. Blessed are they who have not seen yet have believed."

Often today we share Thomas' doubting spirit. Why is it that we are afraid to believe? Why do we often fear even to believe in the Resurrection of Christ, as if some great evil will befall us if we believe? We are poisoned not by our affirmations but by our doubts. Barnum, the famous showman, said: "More people are humbugged by believing too little than too much." It is not Christ who dwells in the tomb, but our spirits, imprisoned by our doubts, our skepticism, our fears.

Come out then! Come out and listen to the Living Lord saying: "Blessed are they that have not seen but who have believed." Faith is the venture into the unknown. We walk into the unknown in company with the Living Lord. He has been through before and now, as our trusted friend, he walks through with us. He knows, as we shall discover, that God reigns over the unknown as well as the known. The light and the dark are both alike to him.

He appeared many other times to the disciples and their friends, to the throng at his ascension. It was this Risen Living Christ after the resurrection who launched the world mission of Christianity. He said: "Go ye into all the world preaching the Gospel." The disciples heard him, recognized him, obeyed him. The evangelization of the whole world by Christian missionaries is not the result of a ghost story but of the Living Christ.

Then he gave them that day the most wonderful promise know to humankind. He said: "Lo, I am with you always, even unto the end of the world." The Lord was with his people. He is with us today. He is among us. It is neither custom nor habit which is the real reason for our gathering Sunday after Sunday to celebrate the Resurrection of our Lord and Savior, cynics notwithstanding. It is the Spirit of the Living Lord among us, blessing our hearts with renewed faith and with that peace of God that passeth all understanding.

The New Testament tells of only one other appearance of the Risen Christ. That was to the Apostle Paul on the Damascus Road. Paul was the persecutor, the doubter, on his way to persecute the Damascus Christians. It changed

He Is Risen

his life. Indeed that meeting changed the history of humankind. It was Paul, the Great Apostle, who took Christianity to Europe. From there it went to England and finally to America. Those of us who are Christians here in America it is because Paul met the Risen Christ on the road to Damascus. Later, in one of his letters, Paul wrote this poignant sentence: "Last of all, he appeared unto me."

"He appeared unto me." All of faith and life is bound in that one sentence. To Paul it meant: "He appeared unto me, the persecutor, the cruel, the undeserving, but he appeared nevertheless and forgave all. He came even to me."

Christianity is not so much a mass movement as a personal adventure with the Living Christ. It is not so much a philosophy of living as the love of God reaching out to each one of us in Christ. He is a personal Lord. He cares about each one as if we alone lived. Each one of our lives is of such infinite value in the love of God that he knows and cares about each one of us, now, today, and throughout eternity. "Last of all, even me." This is our Resurrection Faith.

Listen! "The Jerusalem Daily News" is on the street again with headlines: "Nazarene's Tomb Found Empty!"

"What does the empty tomb mean?" Now we know what it means, and with joy and thanksgiving we join with the chorus of the ages:

"Christ the Lord is Risen Today,
Alleluia,
Sons of men and angels sing,
Alleluia…
And He shall reign forever and ever.
Hallelujah, Amen."

This I Believe

Chapter 20

Uncertainty In Religion

One day a letter came to me asking this question: "Why does God keep me alive and take so many important and better people than I?" The writer was in her early seventies; she had many physical disabilities. She had, according to her own words, no relatives or friends. She had nothing to live for, nothing to look forward to, but an institution for the aged. She ended her letter by saying: "I am alone, as if I were on a desert island."

You can see why a person like that might begin to wonder why God would let her go on living and take a young mother with four children to raise and with the best part of her life still ahead of her, or a child with even more to look forward to.

What I said in answer was essentially this: I don't know why God keeps you alive and takes others, and I doubt if anybody else does. I went on to say that I wasn't at all sure that God was always directly responsible for a person's death. A good many young people today are killed in automobile crashes, and many of these are due to their own recklessness or to the recklessness of their contemporaries. The question is can you blame the results on God?

I remember reading in the papers that a young man was killed in the Pacific Ocean by a shark. I am quite sure that God made both the man and the shark, but I for one would not be willing to say that God deliberately steered the shark out of its normal habitat in the direction of the young man in order to destroy his life.

I also said to the woman who wrote to me that I thought it was God's will for everyone to live out the full length of his of her life the way she had, but, under certain circum-

This I Believe

stances, that doesn't always happen. Why it doesn't I do not presume to know. I then tried, either wisely or unwisely, to encourage her at this particular stage of her life, to think less and do more. Sometimes, of course, our advice would have to be completely reversed. But in her case I tried to tell her that every human being is a desert island until he or she builds a bridge to another island.

I mention this letter not to introduce the subject of life's injustice, or what may seem to us the unfairness of life—why some lives are so empty and others so overflowingly full, why some are so long and others so pathetically brief. What I am interested in is rather the whole business of being able to say, "I don't know," without feeling either like a fool or a failure. That is what I said to her, you see, about the will of God. I said that I did not know what the will of God was in this particular situation, and I said it without feeling that this was a question that I should have been able to answer, especially since I am a minister. In other words, what I should like to have you think about is the place of 'Uncertainty In Religion.' Does it have a place that you don't have to apologize for? And if it does, what is it, and why?

Stop to think for a moment about some of the things that you don't know.

Take pain, for example. Your immediate response is to say: "Well, that is certainly something I know all about. That is what I feel when the dentist begins to drill, or when I slip on the ice and break a bone." But when you stop to think a little more about it, you don't know as much about pain as you may think you do. For instance, why is it that a hypochondriac can feel pain when there is no physical cause of pain, while an athlete suffering from a severe injury may not feel the pain until the game is over? "What is pain?" asks the author of an article on the anatomy of pain. And his answer is: "If doctors could answer the question in precise scientific terms, they might be able to relieve much

Uncertainty In Religion

of the world's misery." In other words, they do not know exactly what pain is; nor do we.

Or take music. Right away you say: "I know what music is. It's a tune that I whistle; a song that I sing, or dance or march to; harmonies that I hear, not only with my ears but also with my soul." Yet, when you stop to think about it, you begin to wonder. Ernest Newman, a veteran music critic, wrote this one time in the Sunday "Times" of London: "Actually we do not know what music is or how it comes into operation when a great composer gets out pen and paper and settles down to his daily chore...The upshot of it all is that we are in the greatest ignorance as to what music is and how the creative musical faculty realizes itself in notes, and by what criteria we decide that one piece of music is more 'inspired' than others."

What makes a wound heal? We don't know. There is a laboratory in the Massachusetts General Hospital that tried for over thirty years to find the answer.

What makes the world go round? We do not know. What is the origin of life? After all the advances that have been made by the geologists and astronomers, and all the theories that have been propounded and all the real knowledge that has been gained, an expert can say that the origin of life is as much a mystery now as it ever was.

In other words, almost everywhere you look there are vast margins of mystery. The only thing you can say when you step over their borders is: "I don't know." If this be true of everything you can think of in life, it is not surprising that you would find the same thing when you come to the greatest of all mysteries, the reality of God.

God's will, what is it? We know something about it, by inference and by revelation. A child knows something about his or her mother's will and learns more every day...One can infer, for instance, from the fact that she is always there when one needs her that she cares about you enormously, and in time of crisis she reveals how much she cares by doing something which makes it unmistakably plain.

So with God. We can infer a great deal about his will from his actions.

He puts us here. We infer from this that he wants us to be here. Furthermore, he has given us a will of our own which can defy his will, and we can infer from this that he wants us to live within a margin of freedom, and that he wants us to learn how to use the freedom he has given us. We know that he has not made life easy for us. There are severe winters and summers that make life difficult for trees and shrubs, and there are storms that only the sturdiest survive. We can infer from that that growth is by friction, as it were, and that flowery beds of ease are not favorable to the growth of human character.

This much we know, but there are still questions that we cannot answer; there are still times when we have to say: "I do not know what God's will is." When a young person dies, is it because God wants him or her to die? My first inclination is to say: "Of course not! Something else has intervened; this is not God's will." But I do not really know. Nor do you.

There are two things I offer now by way of practical advice. The first is quite obvious. Never be afraid or ashamed to say, I don't know if you really don't. Remember that only the stupid are cocksure; that only the ones who know next to nothing think they know it all; and that only the quacks claim to have all the answers.

John Keats put in a word for what he called the faculty of "negative capability." He described it as the capability of "being in uncertainties, mysteries, doubts, without any irritable reaching after fact and reason, of remaining content with half knowledge." Those are his own words. He called this particular faculty, and this I think is an interesting phrase, "diligent indolence." It is something we can afford to cultivate more than we do in religion. Instead of "diligent indolence," we might call it "reverent uncertainty." And Keats emphasized the power of mere passive existence, of receptive pleasure, of conception, incubation, gestation. This is the open heart and mind that waits for God.

In other words, we do not need to apologize for the fact that we don't know everything there is to know about God. As a matter of fact, we do much better if we could cultivate that negative capability of remaining at times content with half knowledge, and being able to say without irritation: "This is something that I don't know yet. I may come to know it sometime, but I do not know the answer now."

The second item of advice is this: the secret of creative living is to be found not in the things we do not know, but in the things we do know. Sometimes we have to be reminded of this, and unless we say this and say it in such a way that it impinges on your imagination, you may gradually slip into the lethargy of ignorance, the lassitude of doubt, and let the fact that you don't know all the answers excuse you from making decisions and taking action.

Keats, you see, could remain content with half knowledge about some things because he had full knowledge about one thing—"a thing of beauty is a joy forever." And he could rest with half knowledge about the rest of things because he knew that one thing.

A child can remain in half knowledge about his or her parents and be completely puzzled and perplexed by many of the things they do if he or she is sure of one thing—that they love him or her. If the child knows that, the child can take in stride their strange behavior that is both bewildering and confusing.

A person of science may be perplexed by the strange behavior of a star or a chemical element which they cannot account for. If, however, that person can say: "I don't know the answer to this, but I do know that the universe is orderly and intelligible," the scientist can then remain safely in uncertainty about a few minor things because they are certain of one great thing.

A religious person finds the secret in the same place. I shall put it now in the first person, not because what I think or feel is of any particular importance, but because I think it makes it easier for one to grasp and translate into their own personal experience.

I don't know how Jesus can be both man and God at the same time. I don't know how that can be. But I do know that in Jesus I find the goal of my humanity and the very ground of my existence; and knowing that one thing, I can remain content in uncertainties about some other things. I don't know exactly what happened to Jesus after his Resurrection. The stories are very confused, and you can feel the tension that was in the air and the excitement that was throbbing through the whole community. Furthermore, I don't know what the writers were trying to say in the stories of his Ascension, or precisely what they meant.

But I do know this. When Lincoln died, people said: "Now he belongs to the ages." When Jesus died, people said: " And now the ages belong to him."

I heard Dr. Henry Sloane Coffin say this in a sermon on Ascension Day back in my Seminary Days. "I do not know exactly what the picture of the Ascension means in terms of geography or astronomy, but I know that in some strange way he reigns over me and over my world; and knowing that one thing, I can remain in uncertainty about the details of the picture."

So, when you begin to wonder about things, as you surely do from time to time, and much more than your neighbors think you do. When you begin to wonder why you go on living year after year while somebody else who seems to be so much more useful is taken, say something like this to yourself: "I don't know why my life should go on;

Uncertainty In Religion

I really don't; and I don't presume to know. But I know that life is precious, and I know that while I have life it is because God gives me that life, and with all my limitations I am going to live it as well as I can."

Jesus in Gethsemane the night before he died, prayed, and he began his prayer this way: "Father, if it be thy will, let this cup pass from me." The implication, you see, is that he didn't know exactly what the will of his Father was: whether it was his will that he should die or that he should live. He didn't know which it was. But he did know that whatever it was, it was good, and that, whether it pleased him or not, he would do it. And he did.

"I know not where the road will lead
I follow day by day,
Or where it ends: I only know
I walk the King's Highway.
I know not if the way is long,
And no one else can say;
But rough or smooth, up hill or down,
I walk the King's Highway."

This I Believe

To order additional copies of **This I Believe**, complete the information below.

Ship to: (please print)

Name _____

Address _____

City, State, Zip _____

Day phone _____

_____ copies of *This I Believe* @ $9.43 each $_____

Florida residents add 6% tax $_____

Postage and handling @ $2.00 per book $_____

Total amount enclosed $_____

Make checks payable to: *H. Burnham Kirkland*

**Send to: H. Burnham Kirkland
2425 Harden Blvd. #265 • Lakeland, FL 33803**

To order additional copies of **This I Believe**, complete the information below.

Ship to: (please print)

Name _____

Address _____

City, State, Zip _____

Day phone _____

_____ copies of *This I Believe* @ $9.43 each $_____

Florida residents add 6% tax $_____

Postage and handling @ $2.00 per book $_____

Total amount enclosed $_____

Make checks payable to: *H. Burnham Kirkland*

**Send to: H. Burnham Kirkland
2425 Harden Blvd. #265 • Lakeland, FL 33803**